flavours of Pro

recipes from the south of France

flavours of **Provence**

recipes from the south of France

Clare Ferguson

photography by Peter Cassidy

RYLAND
PETERS
& SMALL

LONDON NEW YORK

Design, Art Direction and Prop Styling
Steve Painter
Commissioning Editor Julia Charles
Editors Trish Burgess and Ann Baggaley
Production Director Meryl Silbert
Publishing Director Alison Starling

Food Stylist Clare Ferguson
Assistant Food Stylist Marianne Lumb
Researcher Ian Ferguson
Indexer Hilary Bird

First published in hardback in the
United Kingdom in 2007

This paperback edition published in 2009
by Ryland Peters & Small
20–21 Jockey's Fields
London WC1R 4BW
www.rylandpeters.com

10 9 8 7 6 5 4 3 2 1

Text © Clare Ferguson 2007, 2009
Design and photographs
© Ryland Peters & Small 2007, 2009

ISBN: 978 1 84597 853 2

A catalogue record for this book
is available from the British Library.

Printed and bound in China.

Notes

• All spoon measurements are level, unless
otherwise stated.

• Eggs are medium unless otherwise specified.
Uncooked or partially cooked eggs should not
be served to the very old, frail, young children,
pregnant women or those with compromised
immune systems.

• Ovens should be preheated to the specified
temperature. Recipes in this book were tested
using a regular oven. If using a fan-assisted
oven, follow the manufacturer's instructions for
adjusting temperatures.

• All herbs used are fresh unless otherwise
specified.

contents

the flavours of Provence

The gastronomy of Provence is best described as 'cuisines of the sun', a description that conveys the richness and diversity to be found there. Over the centuries, the region and its unique foods and wines have drawn passionate admirers, and still do so today.

The beauty of Provence lies partly in its paradoxical nature. While green and sun-drenched in the fertile south, its interior is wild and rugged, making life there more precarious. The weather is similarly unpredictable: one moment there is blistering heat, soon after come maddening winds, sudden storms, frosts or snow, and these can create feast or famine in equal measure.

Being situated at the crossroads of the Mediterranean, Provence has had a tumultuous history and attracted invaders and visitors alike. Romans, Arabs, Orientals – all have have brought unique contributions to the table. Novel ingredients, unusual seasonings, different cooking techniques, special skills – these are what have enriched the local cuisine, making it a melting-pot of influences, yet still honest, earthy and distinctive in its own right.

Inevitably, cuisines develop from the ingredients locally available. What we now think of as Mediterranean vegetables, such as tomatoes, peppers and squashes, along with white beans and potatoes, were unknown before Columbus brought them back from the Americas. Some of these took centuries to find acceptance, but beans, particularly the white pod variety, have become a staple alongside grains, such as wheat, maize, rye, oats and buckwheat. Other key ingredients produced locally include chickpeas, broad (fava) beans, chestnuts, olives, mushrooms, herbs and wild greens. As animal food was scarce, snails were an important source of protein, and they remain popular, as does wild game.

Of course, food was very seasonal, and supplies often ran low by spring, so the *potager* or kitchen garden was an essential part of every household. Indeed, the traditions of 'growing your own' and eating seasonally remain strong ones in Provence, as they do in many parts of France. Foraging is also valued.

On a larger scale, accessible fertile land occurs only in isolated pockets, so the volume of early and late fruit and vegetables produced in the region is relatively small but famously flavourful. Long summers, multiple harvests and superb market gardens produce foodstuffs of stunning quality and diversity. From Aups come truffles and game; Cannes produces purple potatoes and golden courgette blossoms; scarlet- and white-stemmed chard come from Menton; honeyed melons grow alongside succulent figs in Cavaillon. All the way from the Alps come tiny wild strawberries; artichokes and cardoons grow everywhere; lakes and coastal waters teem with fish and seafood. Who is not inspired by these riches?

Delicate mesclun salad mixtures grow throughout Provence, and many greens grow wild: celery, lovage, borage, nettles, purslane and comfrey are common sights, as are samphire, bay, lemon balm, dandelion, cress, nasturtiums and lamb's lettuce (known as *mâche* or *doucette*). Raw or cooked, these add colour, flavour and nutrients to all sorts of dishes, from soups to salads.

But where would Provençal cooking be without garlic? Like caper buds and leaves, wild garlic leaves often add pungency to dishes, but the cultivated white, pink and purple garlic is considered precious and used with subtlety. Another popular flavour is aniseed, which is found in many dishes, from fish soups to boiled sweets. A popular source of this flavour is fennel, which grows wild. Anchovy is an essential taste.

The ingredient perhaps most associated with Provence, and that figures so large in its cooking, is the olive. Olives are grown in great abundance and pressed to make golden, fruity oil, or preserved in oil that is often flavoured with Provençal herbs. From *pissaladière* to *daube*, few regional dishes are complete without some of the locally produced olives or their oil.

While olive oil is consumed in generous quantities, walnut and pistachio oils also enliven local cuisine. The nuts, too, are eaten as a snack, and chopped or ground for adding to a variety of sweet and savoury dishes.

Fruit is enjoyed raw during much of the year, but some is dried or candied, made into pastes and used in pâtisserie and conserves. The preserved fruits add an enchanting sensuality and prettiness to many desserts, a whiff of summer.

Another distinguishing factor in this region's gastronomy are the floral notes that enhance certain wines and liqueurs, and that flavour many kinds of confectionery, pâtisserie, cordials and jams. Lavender, rose and jasmine are particularly popular, and candied blooms are used with pride by chefs and home cooks. Infusions, such as lime blossom tea, and flower-scented honeys are also used with creative abandon.

Provence has few dairy cows, and therefore little beef, but the dark gamey meat produced from the black bulls in the Carmargue is considered a treat. In the past, beef, veal, lamb and pork were eaten only by the wealthy, but nowadays pork charcuterie is much enjoyed. Chickens, ducks and rabbits flourish in many back gardens, and poultry farming is a lively business. Goats and sheep are reared mainly for their milk, which is made into delectable cheese, but the meat is popular at Easter. Many people still hunt game, such as wild boar, deer and hares; indeed, *la chasse* is an enduring French passion and delicious dishes result.

The Mediterranean diet is healthy and balanced, and nowhere is this better exemplified than in Provence, where food, drink, health and well-being are woven seamlessly together – part of a timeless faith in the natural world.

hors d'oeuvres et casse-croûtes

starters and nibbles

olives, walnuts and their oils

Some 90 per cent of the world's 800 million olive trees surround the Mediterranean, and their produce echoes the *terroir*: it is both complex and superb.

Around May, the trees sprout tiny white flowers that have a faint but delicious scent. The hard little olives appear soon after, changing from pale green to tan, then becoming violet-speckled, brown and finally purplish-black. As the fruit fattens, the stone inside hardens, and the olives are ready for picking between December and February. Deciding exactly how and when to harvest and process them for optimum results requires fine judgement that is acquired only through years of experience.

Table olives

The picked fruit is incredibly bitter in its natural state, and it requires time, ingenuity and creativity to make table-ready. Only 20 per cent of olives are used for this purpose. The remaining ones are pressed into delicious, green-gold oil. Provençal table olives, usually not fermented during conservation, have a fresh, fruity flavour, but a short shelf life of just 4–6 months. Ideally, buy olives loose rather than prepacked, and be sure to smell and taste them first. Store them, preferably covered with olive oil, in a cool, dark place. Use them promptly.

Olive oil

Provence has 3.5 million olive trees, making it the world's 12th largest producer. Most olive oil is consumed locally. Trees do not start bearing fruit until the fifth or sixth year, and it takes 5–8 kg of olives to obtain 1 litre of oil. The trees reach maximum yield in 30 years, but continue fruiting for centuries.

Olive oil, unlike good wine, does not improve with age. It tends to be sharp, distinctive, even peppery when fresh-pressed. Within a few months it mellows, but within a year it deteriorates, so buy it fresh, use it quickly. Finest oils have under 0.5 per cent free acidity.

For 'best', try to buy first cold-pressed, extra virgin olive oil from a named Provençal estate (ideally with the date of pressing noted). Choose one that *you* like, not necessarily one that others favour, and use it for dressing salads, fish and seafood, and for trickling over croûtes. Keep a few other extra virgin olive oils, perhaps blends with slightly softer flavours, for everyday use. Oil labelled simply 'virgin' or 'pure' has had too many pressings and too much chemical intervention to be good for anything except deep-frying. 'Pomace' and lower grades are not culinary grades; they are positively harmful and should be avoided.

There are various ways to get oil from an olive: the modern 'continuous system' uses centrifuges to grind up pulp and spin out oil, which is both fast and economic. The traditional and more artisanal method involves ancient stone presses and water-driven mills to crush the olives. The resulting mash is spread on scourtins: fibrous mats that trap the mash and let liquids pass through.

When decanting the oil, some producers use zinc beakers to scoop out the oil by hand until near the bottom of the container; then they change to a shallow-cupped spatula. This process, called *à la feuille*, keeps the decanted oil free of sediment and is skilful work. Look out for bottles that specify this method; they are marked 'rare produce'.

Most oil is filtered, but murky unfiltered products are deemed more desirable. Some is available throughout Provence, but little is seen worldwide.

Olive varieties

Although olive trees grow well throughout Provence, they are most successful in the higher areas away from the coast, where humidity and insect damage can be problematic. Some varieties are best for oil, others for the table and a few for both purposes. Each area has its favourite variety, and certain areas even have their own AOC label, which is accorded only to the finest produce.

Bouteillan, *Aglandau*, *Caillet Roux*, *Picholine* and *Salonenque* olives yield utterly delicious oil: fruity and buttery or slightly spicy, soft and mellow. Among the best varieties for table olives are *Grossane* (large and firm, often salted or brined), *Luques* (green and full of flavour), *Tanche* (plump, fleshy brown and mild), and *Niçoise* and tiny *Nyons* (perfect for salads and also good for oil).

Avoid uniformly firm, black, pitted olives in brine. These are actually unripe olives that have been dyed with iron-based pigments: a travesty and certainly non-Provençal.

Walnut oil

Provençal walnut trees have always been precious because they have so many uses. Their nuts, and the oil produced from them, are highly valued – real gourmand fare – while their wood is used for making furniture and musical instruments.

It may surprise you to know that walnut oil is second in importance to olive oil in Provence. In fact, in some mountainous regions where walnut trees flourish, olive oil has a history of being 'kept for best'. Walnut oil, called the 'grease of the poor', was for everyday use, along with lard, duck or goose fat, and is still commonly used in these regions, as is butter.

Walnut trees take years to reach maturity, and it requires 6 kg of walnuts in the shell to create 1 litre of oil. The first cold crushing produces the best oil. Further pressings are usually mixed with rapeseed oil to make 'walnut-flavoured oil', which is less desirable than the real thing.

green olive and basil paste
pistounnade de Bandol

While recently visiting Bandol's weekly waterside market, after a rousing glass of chilled Bandol rosé, some salted nuts and olives, we discovered this unusual green olive and basil paste. We found a similar version at Isle-sur-la-Sorgue's famous weekly market, which had tarragon as its flavouring. Both tasted delicious. Try these easy versions spread on crisp biscuits with a glass of something chilled.

250 g green olives stuffed with anchovies in brine or 250 g stoned green olives in brine and 4 canned anchovy fillets
2 garlic cloves, crushed, peeled and chopped
half a handful of fresh basil leaves, torn into pieces
25 g stale bread, wetted and squeezed dry
60 ml extra virgin olive oil
1–2 teaspoons white wine vinegar (optional)
crackers, ficelle toasts, crispbreads or cos lettuce leaves, to serve

Serves 4–6

Put all the ingredients except the oil and vinegar into a food processor. Whizz for 30 seconds.

With the machine running, drizzle in enough olive oil to create a pleasant texture.

Taste, add vinegar to season, if liked, then do a final burst of processing to combine.

Serve with crisp salted crackers, tiny oven-dried ficelle toasts or small crispbreads. Baby cos lettuce leaves are another option.

Variation: If liked, substitute the chopped leaves from 8 stems of fresh French tarragon for the basil, in Isle-sur-la-Sorgue style.

To drink: A glass of pastis, mixed 1 part to 5 with chilled water, will go down well. A herby Italian neutral white wine, a chilled retsina such as Savatiano, or a South African Sauvignon Blanc or some Bandol or Tavel rosé, would all taste excellent.

dried tomato purée
mêlée de tomates sèches

Earthenware bowls containing this deep, rust-red purée, along with a rainbow array of olives and aubergine pastes, are often to be seen in Alpes-Maritimes, particularly around Nice. Maybe it's the Ligurian influence, long-enduring and historic. Made from sun-dried and kiln-dried tomatoes, this paste has an intense, sweet-sharp taste. It can beef up stews and stuffings, enliven soups and sauces, and add new interest to the appetizer tray.

100 g sun-dried or kiln-dried tomatoes
2 tablespoons extra virgin olive oil
4 garlic cloves, crushed and peeled
1 teaspoon coarse salt
½ teaspoon dried oregano or rosemary, crumbled
1 teaspoon fennel or anise seeds
90 ml boiling water or vegetable stock
4 tablespoons dry white wine
crudités, salad leaves, toasts or hard-boiled eggs, to serve

Serves 4

Scissor-snip the tomatoes into small pieces. Heat the olive oil in a frying pan and add the tomatoes.

Pound together the garlic, salt, oregano and fennel seeds using a pestle and mortar. Add to the tomatoes and stir over a high heat until aromatic. Pour in the boiling liquid and cook on a medium heat, stirring, for a further minute, until most of the liquid has evaporated. Turn off the heat. Add the wine, then cover and leave for 5 minutes.

Tip the pan contents into a food processor and whizz until the mixture becomes a rough paste, about 15–20 seconds. Let cool.

Spoon the paste into one or more serving dishes. Smooth the surface and chill.

Serve with crisp crudités, young salad leaves, crunchy toasts or hard-boiled egg halves.

To drink: Try a dry Provençal rosé, an Australian Shiraz rosé or some red Sangiovese. A sun-baked southern Italian red, like Primitivo or an American Zinfandel could be interesting here.

garlic sauce or aïoli
aïoli (et le grand aïoli)

Aïoli is often called the 'butter of Provence'. In an area where butter is little used, and olive and walnut oils predominate, this fabulously dense, stinging, stiff emulsion sauce reigns supreme. Started off in a large pestle and mortar (pounding the garlic, salt and bread aids pungency), it is then finished in a food processor. Make lots: it is infinitely versatile.

Le grand aïoli refers to a whole meal. Around the sauce are arranged poached salt cod (or poached stockfish – wind-dried cod), boiled potatoes, hard-boiled eggs, boiled carrots, broccoli or cauliflower and green beans. Cooked octopus and even roast lamb are sometimes served as part of this grand communal dish on festive days.

Put the salt into a large mortar. Check the garlic and discard any green sprouts. Chop or roughly crush the garlic cloves and add to the mortar. Pound the salt and garlic to a sticky paste with a pestle. Add the softened bread and pound to amalgamate. Now add the yolks and continue pounding to get a thick, golden paste. Transfer this to a food processor.

With the machine running, drizzle in about half the olive oil in a steady stream until the mix has stiffened. Add the lemon juice and continue processing until all the oil has been added and the aïoli is dense, gelatinous and glossy. Finally, add the boiling water to stabilize the emulsion. Serve with a selection of crudités and halves of hard-boiled eggs; use in soups and stews; and spread on toast.

Note: If time is short, put the salt, garlic, bread and egg yolks into a food processor and whizz together. Drizzle in the oil as described above. This gives a lighter, less pungent aïoli.

To drink: Fino sherry, a dry, unwooded white, red or rosé wine, or a Grenache.

1 teaspoon sea salt

8–12 garlic cloves, halved lengthways

25 g white bread, wetted and squeezed dry

2 large, free-range egg yolks, at room temperature

450 ml extra virgin olive oil, at room temperature

freshly squeezed juice of ½ lemon

about 1 tablespoon boiling water

baby vegetables, such as sweet peppers, radishes, fennel and celery, and hard-boiled eggs, to serve

Serves 4–8

tuna spread
thoïonnade

I had tasted something like this spread in a restaurant in Arles, and then I found a recipe in a charming cookbook: Andrée Maureau's *Recipes from Provence*, published by Édisud. This led me in the right direction, and below is my own, slightly different, version. It is truly addictive.

225-g can tuna chunks in olive oil
1 hard-boiled egg, shelled and halved
25 g salted capers, rinsed
25 g salt-cured black olives, stoned
2 garlic cloves, chopped
a small handful of fresh flat leaf parsley, scissor-snipped
oven-dried baguette, crackers, toast, strips of green pepper or hard-boiled egg halves, to serve

Serves 4–6

Drain the tuna, reserving the oil, and put on a chopping board. Add the egg yolk, capers, olives and garlic. Use a hachoir (double-bladed chopper) or cook's knife to rough-chop and combine the ingredients.

Transfer the mixture to a food processor. Pulse 6 or 8 times, then add half the chopped parsley and 5 tablespoons of the reserved oil. Process for 20 seconds. Spoon out into one large serving dish or individual ramekins. Smooth the surface and scatter with the remaining parsley.

Dice the egg white very finely, then make a line of it across the surface of the spread.

Note: This paste also makes a great sandwich filling.

To drink: A Roussanne, a Marsanne or a New World Cabernet Sauvignon.

almond-anchovy paste
saussun de Nice

Almond trees feature strongly in the Provençal hills and valleys, and their nuts underpin many of the regional recipes. In this one, almonds can be replaced by walnuts, or even by breadcrumbs, while verjuice or vinegar can be used instead of lemon juice; just please yourself.

200 g blanched almonds, chopped
6 canned anchovy fillets, or 2 salted anchovies, boned and rinsed
1 small slice of country bread, wetted and squeezed dry
4 tablespoons extra virgin olive oil
2 tablespoons freshly squeezed lemon juice
1 sprig of fresh fennel, dill or tarragon
freshly ground salt and black pepper
salad leaves, olives or saucisson sec, to serve

Serves 4–6

Put the almonds, anchovies, bread and olive oil in a food processor and process for 15 seconds.

With the machine still running, drizzle in the lemon juice until a firm-textured paste results. Add a little iced water to thin the paste, if needed.

Scissor-snip most of the herbs into the paste, reserving a few fronds. Taste, season and stir well.

Transfer the paste to a serving bowl and garnish with the herb fronds. Surround with your chosen accompaniments.

Variation: Roll the paste into 24 or so tiny balls. Serve 4–6 per person in individual bowls, drizzled with some good olive oil.

To drink: A Mauresque or a pastis, or some rosé wine or a chilled fino sherry.

anchovy paste with baby vegetables
anchoïade et crudités

Tiny silver anchovies in all their forms are an essential Provençal ingredient. They season everything from beef steaks to cod and poached eggs with a subtle, savoury saltiness. In the past, bread was rubbed at the table with anchovies, then grilled – the simple basis of this recipe.

4 garlic cloves, crushed
3 teaspoons pissalat or anchovy paste (page 146) or 9 canned anchovy fillets or 3 salted anchovies, boned and rinsed
freshly squeezed juice of ½ lemon
1 large, free-range egg and 2 large, free-range egg yolks
350 ml extra virgin olive oil
1 tablespoon pastis (optional)
raw young vegetables and grilled breads, to serve

Serves 4–6

Put the garlic, anchovy paste and half the lemon juice in a mortar and pound to a thick paste with a pestle.

Transfer to a food processor, add the egg and yolks, and process for 15 seconds.

With the machine still running, drizzle in the olive oil, stopping now and then to scrape down the sides. Continue until all the oil has been added, then add the remaining lemon juice.

Taste the mixture, add the pastis, if liked, then process again briefly.

Note: Anchoïade can also mean an anchovy–garlic–olive oil dip mixture, served warm. It is similar to Piedmontese bagna cauda. Both are loved and both are authentic.

To drink: A white or rosé Bellet wine, or a Bandol; frozen vodka or manzanilla sherry would also be excellent.

black olive paste
tapenade

Black, glossy tapenade gets its name from *tapeña*, the Provençal word for 'caper'. This essential ingredient, along with salted anchovies, canned tuna (optional), garlic, herbs, olive oil, marc or lemon juice or both, creates a heady mix. Use tapenade on toast, and eat with hard-boiled egg halves and raw carrot, celery, fennel, cucumber and tomato. It also makes a good sauce for poached fish or steaks.

350 g dry-cured, soft black olives (to yield 250 g stoned olives)

100 g salted capers, rinsed

6 fresh salted anchovies, boned, rinsed and chopped, or 12 canned anchovy fillets, chopped

50 g canned tuna in brine, drained and flaked

2–4 garlic cloves, crushed

1 teaspoon mixed dried herbs, including thyme, oregano, lavender and savory

½ teaspoon coarse salt

freshly ground black pepper

60–90 ml extra virgin olive oil

1 tablespoon marc de Provence (eau de vie)

freshly squeezed juice of ¼ lemon (optional)

garlicky toasts and rocket leaves, to serve

Serves 4–6

Stone the olives and put in a food processor with the capers, anchovies and tuna. Process, in bursts, to a pulp.

Put the garlic, herbs, salt and pepper into a large mortar, and pound with a pestle to create a pungent paste. Gradually work in the olive pulp, then process in bursts, with the oil, until creamy.

Taste and add the marc and the lemon juice, if liked, for balance.

Drizzle the mixture over garlicky toasts and top with rocket leaves. Alternatively, serve with grilled fish or roast lamb, or mixed into butter for grilled steaks.

Note: These days, green olives, sweet peppers and sun-dried tomatoes often go into so-called tapenades, but black olives create the true classic. In regional markets, the name varies, as does the herb content, colour and texture. Pistounnade (or pistounette in Bandol) contains basil with green olives (see page 12), while the Isle-sur-la-Sorgue version contains tarragon.

To drink: Iced pastis, a chilled aquavit or some marc.

beggar's caviar
caviar d'aubergine

Aubergines of all sizes, colours and shapes are the glory of market stalls throughout Provence; every cook can afford this ingredient. Real sturgeon's caviar is another matter. The joky title of this recipe implies (justifiably) that aubergines are precious in their own right. Local cooks roast them in the oven or over charcoal. I prefer to grill mine directly over gas flames, spiked between two forks.

2 medium aubergines (about 500 g in total)

2 garlic cloves, crushed

3 canned salted anchovy fillets, or 1 teaspoon pissalat or anchovy paste (page 146)

60 ml extra virgin olive oil

sea salt flakes and freshly ground black pepper, to taste

torn fresh basil or scissor-snipped lovage or flat leaf parsley (optional), to garnish

crusty bread or small toasts (croûtes), to serve

Serves 4–6

Preheat the grill and position an oven rack about 7.5 cm below the heat source. Pierce each aubergine six times or so with a fork, then place on the rack. Cook for 10 minutes. Turn over and cook for a further 10 minutes. Alternatively, push kitchen forks into both ends of each aubergine, turn the gas hob to its highest and flame-grill each aubergine, turning at intervals so that they are evenly charred, hot and cooked through, about 6 minutes each. Let cool.

Peel off most of the aubergine skin and discard the leafy stem ends. Drain off any juice.

Put the garlic, anchovies, salt and pepper in a mortar and pound together with a pestle. Add about a quarter of an aubergine and continue to pound.

Transfer the mixture and all the remaining aubergine flesh to a food processor. Pulse briefly in half-a-dozen 5-second bursts, drizzling in the olive oil at intervals. This will create an earthy-textured paste.

Taste and season again. Spoon into a serving dish, sprinkle with your preferred fresh herb, then serve warm or cool, with crusty bread or croûtes.

To drink: Non-vintage dry champagne, or a Pinot Gris or a lightly wooded Chardonnay.

chickpea pancake

socca

This street food snack, still proudly sold in Nice, is made on special flat trays over braziers, and was once the hot breakfast of working men. Today, tourists too eat it with pleasure. Presented as a thin, brown-speckled yellow pancake, frizzly at the edges and gooey in the centre, it is shovelled into paper cones. You add either salt and pepper or sugar, and it is addictively delicious. In other parts of Provence, such as Toulon, a somewhat similar dish, called *La cade,* is made, sometimes served with Pistou (page 66).

200 g chickpea flour (gram flour or besan)
2 teaspoons salt
extra virgin olive oil, for cooking
salt flakes and coarse-ground black pepper or sugar, to serve

Serves 4

In a deep bowl, mix together the chickpea flour and salt. Gradually pour in 500 ml cold water, whisking constantly as you do so. The resulting batter should be the consistency of thin cream. Let stand for 2 minutes.

Heat a large, heavy-based omelette pan or frying pan over a high heat until a drop of water sizzles. Brush olive oil all over it.

Test the batter: if it is too thick, beat in a little extra water and whisk it again.

Spoon 4 or 5 tablespoons of batter into the pan, tilting it so that it spreads evenly.

When the edges have become crisp and the pancake is damp and firm (but not raw) towards the centre, slide it out (this pancake is never flipped over).

Fold each pancake into a fan or wedge shape, then slide into a greaseproof paper circle and stack in a serving basket. Make about 7 more in the same way.

Serve hot, sprinkled with salt and pepper or with sugar. Eat and enjoy: you are tasting some of Provence's ancient history.

To drink: Iced water, or pastis mixed 1 part to 5 with water.

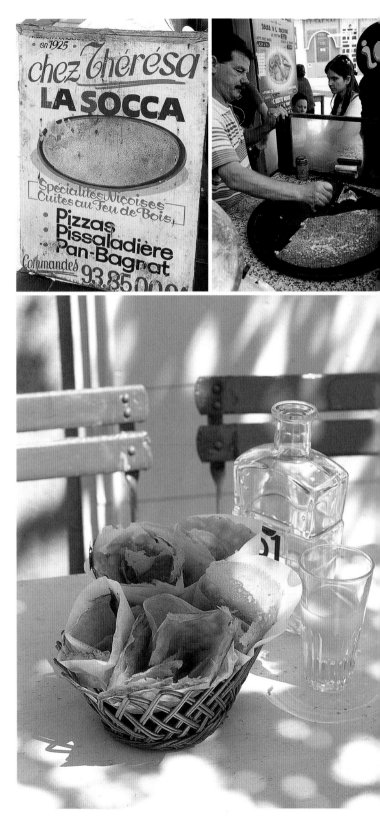

batons of chickpea paste
panisses

In Vieux Nice, down winding market streets, you may see shops selling *pâtes fraîches*. Among the ravioli, gnocchi and pasta on display may be saucer-shaped, golden, glossy discs. These are panisses, which, before cooling, are called *brigadeu*. The hot paste for them, like polenta or porridge, must be beaten with a sturdy whisk; a wooden spoon will not do. Cold panisse, sliced and sautéed until crisp, becomes a tasty snack, like wobbly chips.

750 ml boiling water
1 teaspoon coarse salt
extra virgin olive oil
250 g chickpea flour (gram flour or besan) or farine de maïs (fine polenta)
50 g Gruyère cheese, chopped into small cubes
60–90 ml bacon drippings (optional) or extra virgin olive oil
leafy Batavia, frisée or mesclun salad (see page 36), to serve

Serves 4

Put the boiling water and salt in a large, heavy pan about 25 cm in diameter. Add 2 tablespoons olive oil and return to the boil.

Put the chickpea flour into a bowl, pour in 250 ml cold water and whisk until smooth. Pour this liaison through a fine, ideally nylon, sieve set over a bowl or jug. Rub it all through using the back of a wooden spoon.

Oil 6 or 8 shallow saucers.

When the pan of water is boiling, whisk in the sieved flour mixture in a slow, continuous stream, still over a high heat. Cook and beat for 5 minutes, or until the bubbles start splattering (protect your hand with a cloth). Reduce the heat to medium. Whisk constantly for a further 4–5 minutes, until the mixture begins to pull away from the sides. Beat in the cheese.

Quickly ladle the hot mixture into the oiled saucers. Let cool for 30 minutes, then chill for at least an hour: the panisses grow firmer the longer they stand.

After 6–8 hours, turn them out. Slice into batons or whatever shape you like, and sauté batches of them in a little hot oil or the bacon drippings. Eat as a snack, or serve on top of a green salad.

To drink: Iced water, Sancerre, or dry Riesling.

Swiss chard is a passion of Niçois cooks; you see it sprouting, red-stemmed or yellow-stemmed, in vegetable patches, flower beds and even among the shrubs on traffic roundabouts. Not only is it used with abandon in savoury dishes – omelettes, pastas, stews, soups and casseroles (Niçois folk fondly proclaim themselves *caga-bleias*, 'chard-shitters') – but for desserts and sweets, when it is combined with apple, dried fruits, nuts or honey. It is an all-round useful vegetable. Street food stalls proudly advertise this dish as *torte de blettes*, *torto de bleia* or *tourte de blettes sucré*: a year-round festive treat.

chard tart
tourte de blettes

250 g plain flour

½ teaspoon salt

2 tablespoons extra virgin olive oil, plus extra for greasing

125 ml iced water

sugar syrup, for glazing

olives, to serve

Filling

450 g white-, red- or yellow-stemmed Swiss chard

a handful of fresh flat leaf parsley, chopped

a small handful of fresh basil, torn (optional)

100 g Parmesan cheese, grated

25 g pine nuts, pan-toasted until golden

50 g raisins

1 teaspoon ground cinnamon or allspice, or finely grated lemon zest

4 large eggs, beaten

Sugar syrup glaze

4 tablespoons caster sugar

4 tablespoons water

2 teaspoons lemon juice

a loose-bottomed flan tin or cake tin, 20 cm in diameter

Serves 6–8

Sift the flour and salt into a bowl. Whisk the oil into the iced water with a fork, then stir slowly into the flour. Mix to a firm, dense ball of dough using a knife, cutting and rolling the mixture in the bowl. Turn it out, then pound, roll and knead briefly until smooth. Divide the dough into two equal pieces, wrap in clingfilm and chill for 20 minutes.

Meanwhile, make the filling. Wash and shake dry the chard leaves, then cut into 1-cm strips. Cut the stems into 1-cm pieces. Put all the chard in a bowl with the parsley, basil (if using), cheese, pine nuts, raisins and cinnamon. Mix well.

Flour a work surface and roll out both pieces of pastry – one to a circle 35 cm in diameter, the other to 30 cm. Rub a little olive oil over the flan tin.

Use the larger pastry sheet to line the base of the flan tin, leaving the extra pastry hanging over the sides. Spoon in the chard mixture, mounding it up in the centre. Trickle the eggs evenly over the filling.

Put the smaller pastry sheet on top. Wet the edges of both pastry sheets, pinch together to make a firm seal and roll them inwards, pinching again. Use kitchen scissors to snip into the rim all the way round at 1-cm intervals. Chill for 10 minutes. Meanwhile, preheat the oven to 220°C (425°F) Gas 7.

Bake the tart towards the top of the oven for 30 minutes. Reduce the heat to 190°C (375°F) Gas 5. Make a sugar syrup by boiling the sugar, water and lemon juice together for 3 minutes. Brush the pie with the syrup, and cook for a further 15 minutes, or until browned and fragrant. Remove from the tin and bake for 20 minutes more. Glaze again.

Serve warm or cool in slim wedges as an appetizer, with a few olives.

Note: For a sweeter version, add 1 diced apple macerated in dark rum. Serve this version dusted with icing sugar as a snack or dessert.

To drink: Pastis and water or a fruity rosé wine, or iced water.

The Cours Saleya, Nice's famous food and flower market, is a great place to survey produce, sniff herbs and flowers, enjoy free samples of olives and pastes galore and nibble nuts, nougat or a few slices of *saucisson sec* (offered on the tip of a pocket knife), then sit down at a nearby café and sip a pastis, a *bière picon* (beer and *amer picon,* orange herbal bitters) or a chilled local wine. An order of pissaladière and salad makes a splendid lunch to go with it. This tart is usually sold on a dough base, not unlike pizza. At home, many cooks use bought bread dough or *pâte brisée*, both bought pre-rolled in the local supermarkets for speed. Please yourself which you use.

anchovy and onion tart
pissaladière

1 x 7-g sachet easy-blend dried yeast

1 tablespoon sugar

250 g plain white flour

1 tablespoon milk

150 ml lukewarm water

1 egg, beaten

1–2 tablespoons extra virgin olive oil, for greasing

½ teaspoon salt

Topping

75 g fresh salted anchovies or canned anchovy fillets

6 tablespoons extra virgin olive oil

5 medium onions, sliced into rounds

1 fresh bouquet garni: thyme, parsley and bay, tied together

40–50 small black olives

1 tablespoon thyme leaves

Serves 4

Put the yeast, sugar, 2 tablespoons of the flour, the milk and the water into a food processor fitted with a plastic blade. Let stand for 5–10 minutes, or until frothy.

Add the egg, olive oil, salt and half the remaining flour. Pulse for 1 minute.

Add the remaining flour and pulse again to make a sticky ball of dough. Turn out onto a lightly floured work surface and knead gently for 2 minutes. Put into a deep, lightly oiled bowl. Enclose in a large plastic bag and leave in a warm place for 1 hour.

Meanwhile, separate and bone the anchovies. Slice the fillets lengthways into halves or quarters, depending on thickness.

Heat the 6 tablespoons of olive oil in a large, heavy-based saucepan or frying pan and add the onions. Stir, then add the bouquet garni. Cook over a low, steady heat for 30–40 minutes, until the onions are sweet and mellow but not browned. Discard the bouquet garni and set the pan aside.

Meanwhile, preheat the oven to 220°C (425°F) Gas 7.

Punch down the risen dough. Shape it into a ball, then turn out onto a lightly floured surface and roll it into 1 large oval, circle or square, or 4 small ones.

Scissor-snip, pinch and twist the edges if you like, or roll them under in a plain rim. Dimple the dough with your fingertips, then slide onto a lightly oiled baking sheet. Bake for 8 minutes, or until partly risen.

Scatter the onions over the dough. Create a criss-cross pattern of anchovies on top (see opposite) and put olives in the diamonds. Scatter the extra thyme leaves all over the top. Bake for 10–12 minutes longer. Serve hot.

To drink: A chilled, light red wine like Beaujolais-Villages, a white southern Italian Catarratto or other herby Sicilian white, or chilled amontillado would match well.

squid pasties from Sète
tieilles de Sète

When exploring the Camargue some years ago by boat, my husband and I, in between glorious feasts of oysters, mussels, sardines, mullet and sea bass, kept coming across shops selling small, sturdy, red-stained pies called *tieilles*. Inside were squid, garlic, onions and some local red spice mix. This version uses a ready-made pastry, less dense and doughy than the original, but the effect is much the same. Enjoy these little pies for picnics, meals on the run and snacks. Even smaller versions make great finger food.

400 g shortcrust pastry, chilled
8 small whole squid (about 350 g prepared weight)
3 tablespoons extra virgin olive oil
1 red onion, sliced
50 g fennel, finely sliced
2 shallots, sliced
2 teaspoons seafood spice mix (paprika, chilli, allspice and saffron)
1 tablespoon pastis, for glazing
lemon wedges, to serve

Serves 4

Flour a work surface and roll out the pastry to a thickness of 12 mm. Cut out 8 circles about 12 cm in diameter.

Have ready a four-hole Yorkshire pudding tin (9-cm indentations) or four 9-cm metal flan tins. Push a circle of pastry into each one.

Prepare the squid by pulling the head and the tentacles from the body. Trim off the tentacles below the beak section and discard the rest. Pull out the transparent quill from each squid tube and discard it. Slice the tubes into rings. Halve the tentacle sections.

Heat half the olive oil in a large frying pan and add the onion, fennel, shallots and spice mix. Sauté over a medium heat for 2 minutes. Add the squid and the remaining oil to the pan. Cook, stirring, over a medium heat for 2 minutes more. Let cool.

Spoon a quarter of the filling into each pastry case, reserving about 2 tablespoons of the juice as a glaze. Preheat the oven to 220°C (425°F) Gas 7.

Wet the edges of the remaining pastry circles and put them on top, wet side down. Gently pinch the edges together to seal. Mark with a knife point, if you like, to scallop it.

Bake for 10 minutes, then reduce the heat to 190°C (375°F) Gas 5. Cook for 10 minutes more. Mix the reserved pan juices with the pastis and glaze the tops of the pies. Eat hot, warm or cold, with lemon wedges for squeezing.

Note: No suitable tins? Then set the 8 circles of pastry on a baking sheet. Put an eighth of the filling on each one, then wet the edges, fold over in a half-moon shape and pinch to seal. This makes 8 tiny pastries, so reduce the final cooking time by 5 minutes.

To drink: Pastis mixed 1 part to 5 with iced water, or a crisp New Zealand Sauvignon Blanc or Provençal Picpoul de Pinet.

preserved mullet roe
poutargue

This odd-looking, fishy delicacy, often ignored except by gourmands, is the roe of the grey mullet or muggine. It goes under names such as *mojama*, *mosciamme* or *bottarga*. Sometimes tuna roe is used instead: good, but not the real thing. The mullet roe is washed, dried, salted, pressed repeatedly, then dipped into wax to seal and preserve it. Shavings of poutargue are often bottled and sold in Spanish or Greek delis to season pasta or rice: a disappointment. True poutargue lovers merely cut the lobe horizontally into fine slices, then pull off and discard the wax. They enjoy it as a snack with a drop or two of lemon juice and some freshly ground black pepper, a few olives and a pre-prandial pastis, white wine or some dry Champagne.

aubergine fritters
beignets d'aubergine

Aubergines are celebrated in every sort of dish in Provence: in jams, as sautés, purées and stuffings, as bakes, gratins and loaves, and, as in this recipe, covered with batter and fried. Cutting aubergines into manageable strips makes them easy to eat as finger-food snacks. Serve these with lemon wedges or some fresh tomato coulis, a little Aïoli (page 15), Rouille (page 83) or even some Pistou (page 66).

2 medium aubergines (about 500 g)
1 tablespoon salt
peanut and pure olive oil, for frying

Batter
100 g plain white flour
200 ml cold water (or dry white wine)
1 large egg, lightly beaten
2 tablespoons extra virgin olive oil
2 garlic cloves, chopped

a large, wide pan with a frying basket, for deep-frying

Serves 4

Cut the aubergines into 1-cm rounds. Cut these into 1-cm 'chips' of aubergine: about 100 or so.

Scatter the aubergine chips onto a shallow plate and sprinkle with the salt. Toss and turn them briefly, then leave for 10 minutes.

Heat a 7.5-cm depth of the two oils, mixed 50:50, to about 185°C (365°F) – not quite smoking temperature.

Sift the flour Into a bowl. In a measuring jug whisk the water, egg, the 2 tablespoons of olive oil and the garlic. Pour this mixture into the flour, whisking briskly.

Using kitchen paper, thoroughly pat dry 12–15 chips at a time. Drop them into the batter, turn to coat, and remove using tongs or your fingers. Lower carefully into the oil, one after the other.

Fry for 3–4 minutes, or until crisp outside and lusciously soft within (test one to see). Keep the beignets hot in a preheated oven at 120°C (250°F) Gas ½. Continue frying in batches until all are cooked.

Serve hot, before they lose their crispness, with accompaniments of your choice.

To drink: A crisp Chablis or chilled fino sherry.

tiny liver pâtés in pots
terraieto

Terraieto is an old Provençal word for a small pottery container. The term is also used for the food served in it. This recipe, once steamed and cooled, keeps for up to a week if refrigerated. For a more luxurious version, use cubed duck livers rather than chicken livers, and add a splash of Cointreau as well as the cognac.

150 g chicken livers
2 tablespoons extra virgin olive oil
2 shallots, finely chopped
50 g white bread, wetted and squeezed dry
8 black peppercorns, crushed
8 juniper berries, crushed
½ teaspoon rock salt
4 sprigs each of fresh thyme and fresh marjoram, leaves only
5 tablespoons crème fraîche
2 tablespoons cognac
1 egg, beaten
extra herbs (optional), to garnish
crisp toasts of choice, to serve

Serves 4

Using kitchen scissors, trim the chicken livers, discarding all connective tissue and discoloured parts. Scissor-snip into 2-cm cubes.

Heat the oil in a frying pan, add the shallot and livers, and sauté over a high heat for 2 minutes, until the livers are browned outside, slightly rare inside. Crumble in the bread, then set the pan aside.

Using a pestle and mortar, pound together the peppercorns, juniper, salt and herbs. Stir the mixture into the frying pan and cook for 1 minute.

Transfer the contents of the pan to a food processor and process continuously for about 30 seconds. Add the crème fraîche, Cognac and egg, and whizz again, scraping down the sides once.

Pour the paste into 4 small ramekins and cover with some oiled aluminium foil. Set in a steamer over boiling water, then cover and cook for 12–15 minutes, or until the pâté feels firmly set. Alternatively, put the dishes in a roasting tin and pour in 1 cm boiling water. Cook at 180°C (350°F) Gas 4 for 30 minutes.

Uncover the pots and garnish with extra herbs if you wish. Serve hot, warm or cool with crisp toasts.

To drink: A Loire Cabernet Franc, chilled, or a Merlot.

500 g plain white bread flour

1 x 7-g sachet easy-blend dried yeast

½ teaspoon salt

2 teaspoons sugar

300 ml lukewarm water

3 tablespoons extra virgin olive oil

32 tiny black Nyons olives, or 24 green olives, or crisp-cooked lardons, or a handful of grâtelons (pork scratchings)

Makes 2

ladder breads with olives or pork scratchings
fougasses aux olives et aux grâtelons

All over Provence, from Aups to Antibes, bakeries proudly exhibit their sculpturally stunning breads, from slashed *ficelles*, *bâtardes* and *baguettes* to mountainous *boules de campagne* and *pains au levain*; and twisty batons from curlicues of leftover bread. Wood-fired ovens, traditionally used in bakeries, are a mere memory in many towns, but artisan bakers seem to be thriving nonetheless. Great pleasure is taken in producing local specialities: Lourmarin, for example, has breads containing olives and *grâtelons* (pork scratchings), and oniony and herb-scented versions of *fougasse*, the slashed flat breads typical in Provence. Other places make bread containing anchovies, sage leaves or sun-dried tomatoes. At festival times sweet versions, containing sugar, honey, citrus zests or cinnamon, are popular. This recipe makes two small *fougasses*, suitable for tearing apart and nibbling with an aperitif. The name 'fougasse' probably comes from *focaccia*, derived from the Latin word *focus*, meaning 'hearth'. In the past flat breads like these were often baked in the ashes of the fire.

Put the flour, yeast, salt and sugar into a large bowl and stir twice.

Measure the warm water, add the oil and stir. Pour all but 2 tablespoons of this liquid into the dry ingredients. Mix to form a sticky dough. Punch down the dough and pound to knead it, still in the bowl, four times or until smooth, pinching the edges together and turning it over. Cover with a plastic bag and put in a warm place for 1 hour, or until doubled in size.

Punch the dough to deflate it, then transfer to a lightly floured surface and gently knead it for 2 minutes. Divide into 2 equal pieces. Roll and stretch each piece into an oval about 35 cm long.

Preheat the oven to 220°C (425°F) Gas 7.

Scatter some stoned olives or crispy lardons or pork scratchings on half of each oval. Brush with a little of the remaining oil and water mixture. Fold the other half of the oval over the filling, pat together and roll out again into ovals 35 cm long. Use a sharp knife to make 3 parallel slashes on the left, then 3 on the right (see opposite). Pull the slashes open.

Slide the breads onto two large wetted baking sheets. Bake towards the top of the oven for 20–25 minutes, until golden and crusty.

Note: To make sweet fougasses, the olives or pork can be replaced with citrus zest and orange flower water, or anise seeds and crushed sugar lumps.

To drink: A chilled Crémant de Bourgogne.

The author Colette, who loved Provence with a burning passion, often described local feasts in her evocative novels. Seafood grills, especially those conducted outside over fragrant twigs and charcoal, were a particular pleasure. If you have no French-style outdoor grill, use a barbecue; failing that, you could make one, using four bricks and an oven rack, or simply use an indoor grill: the food will still taste as good. Remember to have lots of lemons for squeezing over the shellfish, and lots of crusty bread for mopping up the juices.

Colette's grilled shellfish
crustacées grillées, façon de Colette

bay, fennel or olive twigs, for the fire
2 large heads of garlic, double foil-wrapped
4 large tiger prawns, halved
4 tiny crayfish or langoustines
4 small crabs (optional)
2 large, preferably spiny, lobster tails
6 lemons

To serve
bunch of flat leaf parsley and/or chervil and/or tarragon
250 ml extra virgin olive oil, in small bowls
freshly ground salt and black pepper
baguettes

a large cast-iron grill with legs, or a barbecue

Serves 4

Set up the barbecue apparatus in a safe place and build up a sufficient depth of charcoal to be able to cook well for 30 minutes. When the coals have burnt down to glowing embers, toss some aromatic herbs on them: bay, fennel or olive twigs work well.

If using an indoor grill, preheat it about 5 minutes before needed.

Oil the garlics, wrap in foil and bury among the charcoal embers just before cooking starts. If grilling indoors, pierce the garlics and poach them, unwrapped, for 20–30 minutes.

Scrub the shellfish under cold running water, then pat dry. Brush the prawns, crayfish and crabs (if using) all over with oil.

Using a heavy-bladed knife, halve the lobster tails lengthways and oil them.

Cut 2 of the lemons in half lengthways.

Once the charcoal is ready, arrange the seafood in groups on the rack, and put the lemon halves alongside them. The small items will cook in 3–5 minutes; the lobster tails (cut side up to start) will take 6–8 minutes and need turning halfway through (use long-handled tongs for this).

Serve the shellfish with some hot garlic cloves slipped from their husks, some fennel dressed with oil, lemon and seasoning, and some herbs scissor-snipped on the spot.

To drink: White or rosé wine from Bandol, or a Bellet, from near Nice. A nice minerally, smoky Sancerre or a meaty white Burgundy are other possibilities.

salades, légumes et graines

salads, vegetables and grains

market gardens

Coastal Provence has an enviable climate, enjoying brilliant sunshine for nine months of the year. This area has a magically extended growing season, which makes it possible to have two or three 'harvests' a year, between March and November.

The Cours Saleya in Nice is possibly one of the most beautiful outdoor produce markets in the world. Gazing at the fantastic array, it is tempting to imagine all of Provence dotted with lush kitchen gardens and picturebook farms all producing enough for each family and community, with enough left over to send to market; but these romantic concepts are not always supported by the facts. Kitchen gardens and small market gardens do make an important contribution, but huge 'factory farms', often using giant greenhouses and hectares of plastic polytunnels, also feature large in the landscape and the economy. Inevitably, *biologique* (organic) methods of production are employed, but ancient biodynamic systems and even hydroponics come into play as well. If you want to find great local produce grown in the traditional way, buy from wayside stalls and tiny village *épiceries* (greengrocers), or visit one of the many excellent farmers' markets. All sell glorious seasonal produce that has a taste of that indigenous *terroir*. There is also a giant wholesale market outside Nice.

Famines, isolation and poverty made staples like chickpeas, cornmeal, chestnuts, olives, rye, spelt-type grains, wild mushrooms, hillside herbs, greens and wild leaf salads, fava beans and some sour wild fruits the mainstays of the Provençal diet. Today, the diet is luxuriously varied.

Food was once strictly seasonal, and supplies often ran low by spring, so resourcefulness was a necessity to keep the wolf from the door. Traditional households kept an attic or cellar well stacked with dried, smoked, salted or distilled comestibles. (Fruit often became alcohol rather than jam because sugar was costly.) Lucky families had a part share of a pig, ritually slaughtered in the autumn and carefully divided up. Used frugally, it enlivened many basic vegetable dishes.

Beans and peas in their many varieties were once the staple foods of Provence, and they are still extremely popular. However, they were somewhat displaced by potatoes in the early 19th century, and these now feature in many dishes. Tomatoes, which seem so quintessentially Provençal, were another import from South America. Now they grow abundantly, becoming wonderfully flavourful in the long hours of summer sun.

Wild and cultivated vegetables, herbs and fruits certainly dominate the flavours of the Provençal kitchen. Olives, capers, squashes, beans, peas, garlic, olive oil, fennel, rosemary, basil, lemon and honey are all integral to the local cuisine, and many of these foods are so delicious that they can be presented very simply. The following pages explore all these foodstuffs and take you through the agricultural year in Provence.

Spring: March, April, May

The gathering of **wild spring greens** begins around March and continues into April and May. Some of these (12, according to tradition) go into the salad mixture called mesclun, which is famous in Nice. This usually comprises rocket, dandelion, hyssop, basil, *trévise* or radicchio, chervil, chicory, frisée (escarole), purslane, *mâche* (corn salad or lamb's lettuce), *feuille de chêne* (oakleaf lettuce) and *sucrine* (crisp baby lettuce). This superb salad, which is now found (much modified) all over the world, is often sold loose in supermarket bins for self-help selection.

Furry **broad bean pods** appear in March, and their tiny beans are delectable eaten raw with sea salt or a sliver of country ham. Bunched **radishes** of two or three types are perfect for dipping into olive oil, then sea salt. Now is also the time for tiny 'eat-all' ***poivrades* (artichokes)**, sometimes called *Violet de Provence*, purplish-green and the size of quails' eggs. These may be eaten raw or deep-fried. Bigger oval artichokes, best boiled or braised, appear later in the spring, followed by the huge round globes of Brittany-style artichokes.

Straggly, purple-green **wild asparagus** shoots are hunted out now and seized with elation. Only the top 20 cm is used, often in scrambled eggs or *baveuse* (dribbly) omelettes. Young **fennel bulbs** are on sale now; in the wild the shoots, flowers and seeds are running rampant by late spring. Marble-sized **new potatoes**, almost translucent, are available March–April. Bunched **spring onions**, **baby leeks** and **wild garlic leaves** can be found on market stalls; cultivated **garlic**, much-prized, appears a bit later.

Marvellous **lettuces** of every size, shape, colour and texture are on sale. Succulent **spring cabbage**, **cucumbers** and **baby onions** flourish.

Baby courgettes, some sold with their yellow blossoms attached, are available by late spring or early summer. *Rabasses* (**wild black truffles**), the same type as the Périgord truffle, can still occasionally be found in mid-March, the season's end. Tender **green asparagus** from the Vaucluse arrives in late February and continues in strength into May. Asparagus from Nice is famous and rarely exported.

Wild hop shoots (*jets de houblon*) and thinnings of **wild garlic** are spring feasts. Once the **wild fennel blooms** are fully out, the blooms, seeds and upper stems may be picked, dried, ground, and used as a green, anise-scented seasoning. Bunched dried fennel stems, sold later, are used to flavour sea bass.

On hillsides and in greenhouses, wild and cultivated **oregano**, **rosemary** and **sage** have mauve blooms, while bay flowers are white; these may be crumbled into salads or into batter for making *beignets* (pages 28 and 49). Raw and cooked **peas**, in and out of the pod, are perfect now. **Haricots**, as well as bigger broad beans, are also in season. **Nettles** and straggly **wild sorrel** for spring soups are high by late April. **Parsley**, **chives**, **chervil**, **dill** and **tarragon** are gathered and used generously, as is **basil**, one of the outstanding symbols of Provençal cuisine.

Morels, those convoluted wild mushrooms that can be light or dark, may appear during April. The hollow caps can be stuffed. Beware the dried Asian lookalikes: they are a disappointment.

Fruit may be in relatively short supply, but **rhubarb** flourishes from March into April.

Summer: June, July, August

Summer in Provence is a glorious season, not least because of its scented fruits. New season's **almonds** in their fluffy green folds, direct from the tree, are on sale from May to June. The tender white nuts, plain or salted, are eaten as a snack, or cooked.

June and July are splendid for **berry fruits**. **Whitecurrants**, **blackcurrants** and **redcurrants** are picked now, at their prime, and used raw in desserts and salads, or made into preserves, sauces and jellies. June brings tiny **wild strawberries** from the woods, mossy banks and lower alps. Their inimitable perfume, intense flavour and short season makes them a celebration. Cultivated pointed **strawberries** are also available, and taste sweet from the intensity of the sun. **Cherries**, white, red and black, are fat and juicy, and perfect for eating by the handful; they are also used in tarts, batter puddings and jams. Smaller fruits, such as **bilberries** and **blueberries**, some of them wild, flourish at this time, as do hairy green and pink-blushed **gooseberries**. Most delicious of all are crimson **raspberries,** now perfectly ripe and scented. These are eaten raw, served in sweet salads or with a cool slice of melon, puréed into sorbets, ice creams or coulis, or made into luscious jam. By August, crimson-dappled **apricots** are piled into baskets, many of them from unsprayed orchards.

By late August, fruit is reaching its glorious peak: late cherries, plus **loganberries** and some early **blackberries,** both wild and cultivated, are to be seen. **Melons**, particularly canteloupes, are at their most abundant; the deep orange flesh, edged with green and pearly white, is outrageously sweet. Cavaillon is particularly famous for its melons. **Plums** also come into their own at this time, appearing in compôtes, jellies, purées and preserves.

Before the scorching Provençal sun reaches its zenith, stalls have **baby carrots**, both orange and yellow: a treat. **Cucumbers** of many varieties, some miniature, others ridged, make perfect salads. Elongated matt **black radishes**, white inside, now make an appearance; believed for centuries to be medicinal, these also make a perfect snack with olives and pastis.

Even more **leafy salads** are now at their peak; market stalls explode with them. Pointed ovals of pink and white **chicory,** called

witloof, is splendid now. Curly pointed heads of *trévise*, along with ruby-coloured balls of **radicchio,** are everywhere. 'Scaroles' (Batavian endives) of many types are bursting out of their boxes. Big-hearted **cabbage** varieties are at their prime, with a few newly introduced Asian greens. Main season **potatoes**, in all colours and shapes, often have their cooking potential explained on their labels. Much discussion ensues when buying. **Sweetcorn** cobs, their soft green husks slightly open to reveal a few dangling silks, draw the crowds. So do early, small white and yellow **aubergines**, **red** and **green chillies**, and fist-sized bunches of **ginger** and **shallots**.

Summer means **tomatoes**, and in Provence they are superb. Although they are often irregular and deeply grooved, the flavour is unbeatable. Some are fatly globe-shaped; others long, almost rectangular. Colours range from acid yellow to green-gold, orange, deep scarlet and purple. Some even have stripes. Those best for eating raw should have a burst of green at the stalk end. For cooking, deep red ripeness is required. Alongside the everyday varieties are tiny scarlet vine tomatoes and larger hothouse varieties. Some may be imports from other parts of France or southern Italy and Spain.

Sweet peppers, which come into full splendour in late summer and autumn, have a magnificent flavour. They also have a variety of colours, including emerald green, yellow, orange, scarlet and purple. They are excellent used raw in salads and cold soups, or cooked in stews, braises, gratins or purées. They may also be roasted, peeled and drizzled with oil, or marinated or pickled for the winter.

The summer **squash** family is by now bountiful. Stripy **marrows**, biggish yellow and green **courgettes**, golden **butternuts**, green and yellow *pâtissons*, like tiny flying saucers, curly **crook-necks** and a wide range of **gourds** are all available.

At this time of year you will find a wealth of **beans**, in pod and out, mature and semi-dried. The range is enormous, and includes scarlet runners, flat and dwarf varieties, **cannellini**, **borlotti** and **coco** bean pods, now whitened and the beans semi-dry.

Yellow- and white-fleshed **peaches,** as well as the red-fleshed variety, which is rather rare, are now available. **Nectarines** are luscious and heavy with scent, and **watermelons** are toppling off the stalls from July into August.

By now, golden **muscat grapes**, soft **green seedless grapes** and dense **black grapes,** with a bloom like velvet, appear in the markets. Look out too for **mauve grapes,** such as *chasselas*, which are bursting with juice and flavour.

Ox-heart **cherries** are now at their peak, and late summer sees figs for sale – white (green) and black (purple) types – often with leaves and twigs still attached. Green olives for brining may show up from late August into September.

Autumn: September, October, November

The onset of autumn rains and cooler days heralds the start of the **wild mushroom** season. September–October is when collectors, baskets on their arms, will be seen intently studying the ground. It pays to be knowledgeable, as every year in France some accidental poisonings occur. So strong is the tradition of mushroom-picking, however, that people are not deterred. For this reason, French pharmacies must by law offer free advice about the edibility of what people have collected.

The **French cep** (*Boletus edulis*) is the prize fungus – dense, meaty and handsome, with a heady aroma. Also cherished are saffron-coloured **milk caps** (*Safrane lactarious delicious*) and two types of **chanterelles** (*Girolles canthorellus cibarious* and *G. c. infundibuliformis*). Fragile, black **horn of plenty mushrooms** (*Croterellus cornucopoides*), commonly called *trompettes de la mort* (trumpets of death) – and safe to eat, despite their name – crop up too. Rare, lovely and orange-hued **Caesar's mushrooms** (*Amanita caesaria*) may sometimes be found, which is a cause for celebration. Tiny, leggy **golden mushrooms** growing in rings are often simply called *mousserons*, and will be gathered and cooked with sautéed chicken, wine and cream. Other varieties widely found and gathered include black, umbrella-shaped **field mushrooms**, *champignons de Paris*, the French equivalent of English button mushrooms, **honey fungus** and **tree ears**.

Autumn is the time for harvesting **grains**, and Provence has these in abundance. **Maize** is particularly important, as it feeds

both people and animals. **Buckwheat, oats, wheat, spelt, rye, millet** and **barley** go mostly to the mills for grinding into flour or meal; some will be cracked or crushed, or part-cooked and turned into semolina, couscous and bulgur.

September brings **walnuts, chestnuts** and **hazelnuts**, which continue for months. Other important nuts, **almonds** and **pistachios** can also be found on sale.

Quinces and **crab apples** are prominent in the markets. So, too, are crisp apples, red, green and striped, some for cooking, some for the table. **Pears** continue to flourish, **plums** are everywhere, and **greengages** (*reines-claudes*) are considered particularly fine. **Kaki** or **persimmons** look like orange gems on the leafless trees, and their curious flavour is much appreciated. Wild and cultivated **blackberries** are now widely available.

Leeks are at their peak during September, and **onions** can be bought in splendid tresses. Beans and peas, in and out of the pods, fresh, dried, used puréed or dried and ground to meal, as well as chickpeas, an ancient mainstay of the Provençal diet, are always available.

Winter: November, December, January, February

During these colder months, which may bring frost, sleet or snow, Provençal markets are still crammed with superb produce. Dark crinkly winter **cabbages, rape, cauliflowers,** green and purple **sprouting broccoli,** the hardier **escaroles** (like Batavian endive), **spinach beet** and **spinach,** are the belles of the vegetable stands. Celery, **carrots, turnips, swede, thyme** and **sage** can be found bundled up for soups.

Cavolo nero, a long, dark winter cabbage from nearby Italy, is often sold beside stalls bursting with the many types of **Swiss chard**. Most chard is white-stemmed, but some types have red, scarlet or yellow stems. The green tops and the stems taste different from one another, but both are good. The Niçois are besotted with Swiss chard; they define themselves by it.

Pomegranates, round, red and luscious, are perfect now. Cut them in half, squeeze like lemons and drink the juice over ice with marc and a stick of cinnamon for a cocktail sensation.

Now **olives** begin to be harvested for oil and for eating whole; there are many different types. The markets sell these bitter green-brown new olives to be aromatized back at home.

Chestnuts are gathered and roasted in open hearths using symmetrically punctured pans that allow each nut to be easily positioned. Dried, smoked or cracked and ground, these will become chestnut flour, but the best, most perfect ones are infused with vanilla sugar to be sold as sweets – *marrons glacés*.

Thanks to the long extended warm season, all sorts of **citrus fruits** remain available throughout the year. Left on the trees, they can be picked to order. The large, thick-pithed local yellow citrus fruits (citrons or *cédrats*) are crystallized – a famous Riviera delicacy. **Lemons** of many kinds (each of the four seasons has a variety) are celebrated in Menton in a giant carnival each spring. Citrus juices, zests, essences, preserves, confits and jams are an essential part of life in Provence.

In November the **wild black truffle** season begins. There are no local white truffles. Black truffles are called *rabasses* in much of Provence, and those who hunt them are known as *rabasseurs*. Truffles are fungi that grow close to the roots of oaks and sometimes elms, so are relatively difficult to locate. Clouds of tiny flies may signal a possible site, but the best system is to use a trained truffle hound. The pheromone-like aroma of black truffles excites the dog, which will bark, nuzzle and try to dig it up. Pigs, once traditionally used for truffle-hunting, are less used now because they tend to gobble up their find.

Whole truffles, brushed clean and stored in crumpled paper, can be put among some whole eggs or into white rice for their pungent aroma to infuse them: delicious. Sliced wafer-thin on a purpose-made miniature mandoline, truffles can be added to soft-cooked egg dishes, plain white pasta, creamy risotto or buttery boiled potatoes. Poached whole in a little rich chicken essence, they can also be eaten whole, like potatoes, in the old way of country people and gourmands.

Dates and times for Provençal truffle markets can be found at www.provenceweb.fr (see page 157); Richerenches, Carpentras, Apt, Uzès and Valtréas are truffle centres worth investigating.

This is probably one of the world's best-known (but least well-made) salads. Found everywhere from seaside cafés to smart restaurants, and from mountain hostelries to late-night clubs, it is rarely fresh or authentic. Debate rages over its provenance, but certain facts about its content seem immutable: anchovy fillets and canned, good-quality tuna are vital, as are hard-boiled eggs. Also essential are tomatoes, cucumber, green pepper, onion, raw broad beans and basil leaves, while tender baby artichokes, ideally raw, are desirable. Black olives are optional, but usual. No cooked vegetables whatsoever are allowed. The garlic is best rubbed around the bowl, but it can also be crushed into the olive oil and lemon dressing poured over the salad. (However, many maintain that lemon is not permissible.) Think of this salad as a celebration of fresh flavours.

salad and sandwich from Nice
salade niçoise et pan bagnat

2 garlic cloves, lightly crushed and halved

1 head of cos lettuce, or ½ head of Batavia or frisée

1 small gem lettuce or other crisp baby lettuce (optional)

2 spring onions, sliced

250–350 g good-quality canned tuna pieces or cooked, cold, fresh tuna

50 g salted anchovies or 24 canned salted anchovy fillets

24 black olives, Niçoise type (optional)

3 or 4 hard-boiled eggs, shelled and quartered or halved

a handful of fresh, small basil leaves, roughly torn

200 g fresh broad beans, podded and peeled

2 ripe red tomatoes, each cut into 6 or 8 wedges

10-cm piece of cucumber, peeled and cubed

2 fresh baby artichokes, trimmed, halved and chokes removed (or canned equivalent)

4 radishes, sliced

8 tablespoons extra virgin olive oil

½ teaspoon sea salt flakes

1 lemon, cut into wedges (optional)

Serves 4–6

Rub the garlic cloves around the base and sides of each salad plate or bowl.

Wash and shake dry the salad leaves, then cover and chill. Tear them and use some of each type to line the plates or bowls. Scatter in some spring onions.

Break the tuna into coarse chunks and place on the lettuce. Rinse and dry the anchovies if very salty, then arrange in a criss-cross pattern on the tuna. Add the olives (if using), eggs and basil. Dot with the broad beans, tomatoes, cucumber, artichokes and radishes.

Whisk together the oil and the salt, adding the juice from 1 lemon wedge (if using). Drizzle this dressing over the salad just before serving, and put a wedge of lemon on each plate, if liked.

Note: If broad beans are not available, break the rules and substitute 150 g briefly cooked French beans.

To drink: A robust red wine, such as a Gigondas, an AOC Provençal rosé, a Bordeaux rosé or a chilled, dry Riesling.

Pan bagnat
This splendid dish, literally 'bathed bread' (from tomato juices and dressing), is essentially salade Niçoise packed into a large round *boule* or country loaf, the middle of which has been scooped out. It can also be made with lengths of hollowed-out baguette. The bread is pressed flat, wrapped in greaseproof paper, tied up and a weight placed on top. In 2–3 hours it is ready to unwrap and eat.

Cut pan bagnat looks gloriously colourful, like a layered terrine. Defying convention, I add anchovy-stuffed green olives to mine, and sometimes wafer-thin layers of saucisson sec or some slices of cured raw ham. I also increase the amount of dressing. This is a wonderful picnic dish, best followed by some scented melon for dessert.

Tomatoes, though integral to Provençal cuisine, were only introduced into Europe after Columbus made his epic voyages. No cookbook of the Ligurian region mentions them until 1839, and it seems that only after commercial promotion of canned tomatoes during the early 1900s (supported by the famed local chef Auguste Escoffier) did the locals take to them. Even now, many Italian and Provençal cooks add a little sugar to tomato dishes to counteract what they say is too acidic a taste. In fact, all the key Mediterranean vegetables – tomatoes, sweet peppers, courgettes, squashes, white beans and potatoes – are relative latecomers to the area, but how they've been celebrated since! This dish, cooked on top of the stove, produces almost confit-style tomatoes; the more usual way is to oven-bake them. However, this homely method is so easy, especially for households without an oven, and luscious too.

Provençal tomatoes
tomates à la provençale

6 medium ripe, flavourful tomatoes, halved horizontally

1 teaspoon salt

1 teaspoon caster sugar

8 black peppercorns

¼ nutmeg, freshly grated

2 shallots, finely chopped

2 tablespoons extra virgin olive oil

2 garlic cloves, crushed or chopped

a handful of chopped mixed fresh herbs, such as chives, parsley, tarragon, borage, oregano and sage, or 2 teaspoons Provençal mixed dried herbs (if no fresh available)

3–4 tablespoons water or stock or white wine

3 tablespoons breadcrumbs, pan-sizzled in 1 tablespoon extra virgin olive oil

Serves 4

Scoop out and discard the seeds and juice from the tomatoes (or reserve for use another time).

Using a pestle and mortar, grind together the salt, sugar and peppercorns. Stir in the nutmeg. Sprinkle the tomatoes with this mixture, and put some shallots inside each one.

Pour the olive oil into a large, wide, heavy-based frying pan and heat hard for 2 minutes. Add the tomatoes in a single layer, hollow side up. Scatter in the garlic and half the herbs, then cook for 2 minutes on a fairly high heat, uncovered.

Now add 2 tablespoons of the water, stock or wine. Cover the pan, reduce the heat to its lowest setting and cook for 10 minutes more.

Use a spoon and palette knife to turn the tomatoes, being careful to keep neat shapes. If the liquid is gone, add 2 more tablespoons of the water, stock or wine. Cover the pan again and continue cooking for 10 minutes more. By now the tomatoes should be sticky, nearly collapsed and very fragrant.

Serve them right side up, with any of the sticky reside from the pan, and sprinkled with the remaining fresh herbs and a few toasted breadcrumbs, if liked. Enjoy hot, warm or cool.

To drink: Pastis mixed 1 part to 5 with iced water, a chilled Aquavit or iced water.

mixed bean salad
mélange de haricots et coco-plats

Names of pod beans in Provence can be completely mystifying to most of us: *haricots*, *haricots verts*, *cocos*, *coco-plats*... Varieties include green, striped, freckled, gold, rosy, shocking pink and faded yellow. This recipe mixes different-coloured beans – those with pods tender enough to eat, and those that must be podded first and used peeled or unpeeled.

300 g fine green beans, trimmed
100 g fresh, canned or frozen podded beans, such as broad beans, haricots, coco-plats, or borlotti
100 g flat and flexible green beans, such as stringless or Romano beans, or yellow wax beans
1 teaspoon sea salt flakes
6 garlic cloves, unpeeled
2 shallots, peeled
1 sugar lump or 1 teaspoon sugar
2 tablespoons extra virgin olive oil
2 tablespoons walnut oil
8 walnut halves, chopped
4 spring onions, thinly sliced

Serves 4–6

Halve all the green beans and the podded beans. Peel the broad beans if you prefer.

Put them into a large, deep saucepan with the salt, 150 ml boiling water, the garlic, shallots and sugar. Bring to boiling point, then reduce the heat and cook for 6–10 minutes, or until the beans taste tender. Use tongs to transfer to a serving dish.

Add the shelled beans to the pan. Cook for 2–3 minutes until brilliantly colourful and tender to the bite. Remove and chop or mash the shallots. Transfer to the serving dish.

Boil the liquid down to about 4 tablespoons. Remove the garlic cloves, peel them and squeeze their soft purée into the liquid. Stir in the oils, nuts and spring onions. Pour the finished sauce over the beans and serve.

Note: Although lemon juice is not essential, it can be added to the dressing if you like. Alternatively, add a splash of white wine vinegar.

When young and green, podded coco-plat beans can be eaten raw or lightly cooked. Once the pods turn dry, white or yellow, the beans inside must be treated like dried ones and given long, slow cooking.

To drink: A Pinot Grigio or an unwooded Chardonnay.

broad bean salad
salade de fèves

All around the Riviera, beans are treated with affection and respect. Broad beans (fava beans) have always been a major part of the diet in this area. When young, they are often podded, added to salads or simply eaten raw with a sliver of goats' or sheep's cheese as a snack. Older beans are skinned and briefly cooked, then drizzled with oil and sprinkled with garlic and herbs, or used in soups and stews.

800 g fresh broad beans in the pod (or 350 g frozen ones)
4 baby leeks or large spring onions, diagonally sliced
4 garlic cloves, chopped
3 teaspoons sea salt crystals
½ teaspoon rough-crushed black peppercorns
2 tablespoons lemon juice, verjuice or dry white wine
8 sprigs of fresh thyme or savory
a small handful of fresh chives
a small handful of fresh curly parsley
a small handful of fresh mint or lemon balm
8 tablespoons extra virgin olive oil

Serves 4

Pod the fresh broad beans and peel them. Put them (or the frozen beans) into a saucepan, half-cover with boiling water and return to the boil. Reduce the heat, cover and cook for 2 minutes.

Add the leeks and cook for 2 minutes more. Drain off most of the liquid, but reserve 1–2 tablespoonfuls.

If using frozen beans, pinch off the skins. Return them to the pan.

Meanwhile, put the garlic, salt, peppercorns and lemon juice into a large mortar and pound to a paste with a pestle. Scissor-snip the herbs into the paste, reserving a few bits of each for garnish. Add the reserved bean cooking liquid.

Stir in the olive oil, then pour the contents of the mortar over the salad. Mix gently and spoon into a serving dish, top with the reserved herbs and eat warm.

To drink: Sancerre or a Sauvignon Blanc, Loire or otherwise.

two-pepper salad
marinés

... abound in Provence. They come in all shapes and sizes (often wildly irregular), and many colours, including pale green, emerald green, orange, red, yellow, tiger-striped and purple-black. When chargrilled and eaten with country bread rubbed with garlic and herbs, they're simply heavenly.

3 large, ripe red sweet peppers
3 large, ripe yellow sweet peppers
7 tablespoons extra virgin olive oil
juice and grated zest of 1 bitter orange or lemon
1 teaspoon pissalat or anchovy paste (page 146), or 2 canned anchovy fillets, chopped
2–3 tablespoons salted capers, chopped
a small handful of fresh basil, torn
salt and freshly ground black pepper
4 slices of thick toast, rubbed with crushed garlic, to serve

Serves 4

Preheat the grill to its hottest temperature.

Rub the peppers lightly with 1 tablespoon of the olive oil, put them on a rack with their stems facing outwards and place under the grill. Let them roast until they blister and sizzle, giving them a 45-degree turn every 4–5 minutes. Continue until they are tender and charred: about 20 minutes.

Transfer the peppers to a plastic bag and seal tightly. Let stand for 5 minutes or longer.

Remove the peppers and use kitchen paper to help pull and slide off the skins. (Avoid holding under the tap, as too much sticky juice will be lost.) Once skinned, remove the stems, seeds and membranes. Slice the flesh and arrange on a serving plate.

Put the orange juice, half the zest, the anchovy paste, capers and a tablespoon of the remaining olive oil in a mortar. Pound together with a pestle, then taste and adjust the seasoning.

Stir in the remaining 5 tablespoons of olive oil. Spoon this dressing over the peppers, then scatter the basil and remaining zest on top.

Serve on garlicky toasts.

To drink: New World rosé or an off-dry Zinfandel.

stuffed baby vegetables
petits farcis

Stuffing vegetables transforms them. Use lots of fresh herbs, not dried ones.

4 medium cap mushrooms or 4 medium ceps, lactaires or blewits, with stems
4 medium salad tomatoes or 4 large plum tomatoes
2 small courgettes or 8 pâtissons (round squashes)
4 Swiss chard stems
2 large globe artichokes or 4 small ones
1 lemon, halved

Stuffing

4 tablespoons extra virgin olive oil, plus extra for drizzling
25 g stale bread, crumbled or diced
2 garlic cloves, chopped, and 1 onion, finely chopped
a handful of fresh mixed herbs, such as dill or marjoram, chives, parsley, borage and basil, leaves only, scissor-snipped
8 allspice berries, 12 black peppercorns and 12 coriander seeds
½–1 teaspoon rock salt or gros sel
75 g cooked chicken or ham, or saucisson sec, chopped
100 g bacon cubes, browned and chopped

Serves 4

Preheat the oven to 180°C (350°F) Gas 4. Hollow out the mushrooms, tomatoes and courgettes, reserving all the flesh and trimmings. Keep the tops of the tomatoes (and squashes, if using) as lids. Quarter the chard stems. Put the vegetables in a large, lightly oiled roasting tin.

Discard the artichoke stems and the two lowest rows of outer leaves. Scissor-trim the remaining leaves down to 4 cm from the base. Use a spoon melon baller to dig out the fluffy choke and yellow inner leaves. Discard both. If using large artichokes, halve them lengthways and rub with the lemon. Blanch in boiling water for 2–3 minutes, then drain.

Heat the olive oil in a frying pan, add the breadcrumbs, garlic and onion and cook on a high heat, stirring, for 3 minutes. Chop the reserved vegetable trimmings, add to the pan and cook for 10 minutes more. Add the fresh herbs.

Grind the allspice, pepper and coriander with the salt. Combine with the breadcrumb mixture and cooked meat. Taste and season.

Fill the hollowed-out vegetables neatly and replace the lids. Drizzle generously with olive oil. Bake, uncovered, for 25 minutes.

To drink: A Pinot Grigio or a young white Rioja.

Courgettes, along with a colourful array of gourds and squashes in a multitude of shapes, make gloriously exuberant displays throughout the summer, autumn and winter. These are important vegetables in Provençal households. Before the courgettes are harvested, they produce silky yellow blossoms that sit among the serpentine tangle of stems and leaves, and seem to smile at the sun. The female flowers develop into little courgettes; use these when the flowers are large, and eat both parts. This is a celebration dish, since courgette flowers are scarce and therefore expensive. Lucky are the gardeners who have courgette flowers in their vegetable patch.

courgette blossom fritters
beignets de fleurs de courgettes

12 female courgette flowers with courgettes attached

Stuffing

50 g pine nuts, pan-toasted and chopped

50 g stale bread, crumbled

6 salted anchovy fillets, chopped

50 g medium-hard goats' cheese, grated or crumbled

25 g fresh chervil, chives or parsley, scissor-snipped

2 teaspoons pastis or fresh lemon juice

5-cm depth of grapeseed oil and virgin olive oil, for frying

Batter

125 g plain white flour

a few pinches of salt and freshly ground black pepper

1 tablespoon extra virgin olive oil

180 ml lager or beer

2 large eggs, separated

2 garlic cloves, finely chopped

2 sprigs of fresh chervil, chives or parsley, scissor-snipped

Serves 4

Check the flowers inside and out for caterpillars. Discard the pistil, the central part inside the flower that consists of the ovary, stigma and style. (Doing this makes room for the stuffing.)

Put all the stuffing ingredients on a board and chop together, using a hachoir (double-bladed knife). Alternatively, put the ingredients into a food processor and pulse in brief bursts. Sprinkle the pastis or lemon juice on top of the mixture.

Put 2 teaspoonfuls of stuffing inside each flower. Close the petals by twisting them, or tying them together with fine string or a chive stalk.

Pour a 50:50 mixture of the two oils into a large, deep frying pan or a deep-fat fryer and heat to 190°C (375°F), or until a cube of bread added to the pan turns brown in 10 seconds.

Meanwhile, make the batter. Sift the flour and salt and pepper into a bowl. Add the tablespoon of olive oil, the lager and egg yolks, and whisk briefly to combine. Stir in the garlic and snipped herbs.

In a separate bowl, whisk the egg whites until soft peaks form. Fold them into the batter.

Carefully dip each stuffed flower into the batter to coat it. Let any excess batter drip back in the bowl.

Fry in the hot oil in batches of 4 or 5 for 3 minutes, turning them over halfway through. Transfer to a moderate oven to keep hot while you finish cooking the remainder. Eat hot.

To drink: A Sauvignon Blanc such as Sancerre or a Loire Sauvignon Blanc.

potatoes stewed with olives
pommes de terre aux olives

Potatoes reached the French Riviera in the 1560s, but they were appreciated mainly for their decorative flowers, not as food. Napoleon's soldiers probably helped to popularize them because potatoes roasted in the embers were basic survival fare. This recipe seems particularly Provençal, and is absolutely delicious. It is especially good served with game.

500 g walnut-sized new potatoes, such as charlottes, rattes or Belles de Fontenoy, scrubbed

4 tablespoons extra virgin olive oil

4 garlic cloves, chopped

2 teaspoons fennel seeds or anise seeds

350 ml medium-dry white wine

100 g salt-cured black olives

50 g anchovy-stuffed green olives or 40 g green olives and 2 anchovy fillets, chopped

sea salt flakes and freshly ground black pepper

Serves 4

Dry the potatoes and halve them crossways. Heat the olive oil in a large frying pan or flameproof casserole, add the potatoes, cut side down, and sauté for 5 minutes, until sizzling. Add the garlic and fennel seeds, then shake the pan and stir over a medium heat for 30 seconds, or until aromatic.

Pour in the wine and add salt and pepper, then cover the pan and cook on a very low heat, undisturbed, for 15 minutes.

Add the two kinds of olives, shake the pan, then cover and cook again for a further 20 minutes, or until most of the liquid is gone, and the olives and potatoes are unctuously tender and aromatic.

Remove the potatoes and olives and keep warm. Boil the liquid for about 5 minutes, or until reduced by half. Season to taste. Return the potatoes and olives to the pan and heat through.

Serve plain or spooned over a green salad, or use to accompany baked fish, roasted poultry or feathered game.

Note: If you use *pommes truffes* (truffle potatoes), such as black congo or *truffes de chine*, which are knobbly and purple-fleshed, you will create a truly exotic mélange.

To drink: A southern French red such as Grenache, a Spanish Garnacha or a Chianti.

aubergine, onion and courgette stew
bohémienne

Also called *boumanio*, this dish could be described as ratatouille's little-known sister. According to Jacques Médecin, a gourmand and former mayor of Nice, ratatouille 'requires long and difficult preparation' because the vegetables must be sautéed separately, then combined in a rich tomato sauce. This simpler vegetable stew is delicious hot or cold, and tastes great the following day.

6–8 tablespoons extra virgin olive oil, plus extra if needed

6 garlic cloves, chopped

2 medium onions, sliced

350 g ripe, flavourful tomatoes, chopped

a handful of fresh thyme sprigs

100 ml fresh tomato juice or passata

4 medium courgettes, sliced

1 medium aubergine, diced into 1-cm cubes

50 g Gruyère or tomme (goats') cheese, grated

a small handful of fresh flat leaf parsley, scissor-snipped

sea salt flakes and freshly ground black pepper

Serves 4

Heat 2 tablespoons of the olive oil in a large, heavy-based pan or flameproof casserole. Add the garlic and onions, then the tomatoes, seasoning and thyme. Cook, stirring and mashing over a high heat, to create a rich, thick tomato sauce. Stir in the tomato juice, then transfer to a bowl and set aside.

Wash and dry the pan, then heat 2 more tablespoons of the oil. Sauté the courgettes, turning often, until soft and golden: about 2–3 minutes. Using a slotted spoon, add them to the sauce.

Heat another 2 tablespoons of oil in the pan. Add the aubergine and sauté over a high heat, stirring until tender and translucent. If necessary, add 2 or more tablespoons of oil to the pan.

Tip the tomato sauce back into the pan. Reheat gently, covered, for 10–12 minutes. Taste, season and serve sprinkled with grated cheese and snipped parsley.

Note: For ratatouille, sauté 2 chopped red sweet peppers and 1 chopped green sweet pepper for 5–6 minutes after the aubergines. Combine as described above.

To drink: A crisp rosé, well chilled.

Camargue rice salad
salade du riz camarguaise

Last February, at the end of a glorious sojourn in the Luberon, we drove through the strange flatlands of the Camargue to Saintes-Maries-de-la-Mer, pilgrimage place of Europe's Romany peoples. Past rice fields, black bulls, white horses and bare grape vines, we came to the traditional thatched dwellings of the *gardians* (cowboys). We ended up staying in one, surrounded by reed beds, lagoons and silence. That night we ate an excellent beef stew. With it came rice a little like this, which is good enough to be served on its own as a warm salad.

50 g salted butter
2 red onions, sliced
200 g Camargue red rice, washed and drained
100 g Camargue or other long-grain white rice, washed and drained
1 fresh bouquet garni: thyme, sage, bay and oregano, tied together
2 dried chillies, crushed but whole
freshly squeezed juice and finely grated zest of 1 orange
freshly squeezed juice and finely grated zest of 1 lemon
1½ teaspoons sel de la Camargue or other good sea salt
50 g baby capers (nonpareils)
50 g green or black taggiasca olives
2 tablespoons concentrated chicken bouillon or
1 stock cube, crumbled

Serves 4–6

Heat a heavy-based flameproof casserole and melt the butter. Sauté the red onions over a high heat for 2 minutes.

In a separate pan, bring 400 ml of water to the boil, add the red rice and return to the boil. Reduce the heat to a simmer, cover the pan and cook for 25–30 minutes, or until the rice is *al dente*.

Scatter the white rice and all the remaining ingredients (reserving a little zest) into the pan with the onions. Add 200 ml boiling water.

Return to the boil, then simmer, covered, for 10–12 minutes, or until the rice is tender and all the liquid has been absorbed. Remove the bouquet garni and chillies. Stir in the cooked red rice.

To serve, pile up the rice, scatter with the reserved citrus zests and eat as a warm salad. Alternatively, serve cool or cold.

To drink: An earthy, nutty white Rhône or an older Chardonnay.

vegetable couscous
couscous aux legumes

North African-style couscous is found in Italy and eastern reaches of the Provençal coast, probably introduced by Arab invaders. The argan oil in which the vegetables are cooked comes from North Africa. It has an earthy flavour and is sold in specialist delis and ethnic stores.

350 g 'instant' couscous
500 ml boiling vegetable stock or water
2 tablespoons extra virgin olive oil
2 tablespoons argan, walnut or chilli oil
5-cm piece of fresh ginger, sliced lengthways and shredded
8 garlic cloves, unpeeled and lightly crushed
8 cardamom pods, lightly crushed
2 cinnamon sticks, lightly crushed
2 teaspoons cumin seeds
750 g assorted vegetables, such as carrots, sweet potatoes, onions, celery, courgettes, parsnip or salsify, cut into 1-cm pieces
75 g sultanas
rock salt and freshly ground black pepper
fresh mint or coriander leaves, to garnish
150 ml harissa paste (optional), to serve

Serves 4–6

Put the couscous into a medium heatproof bowl and add about half the boiling stock: it should cover the couscous by 1 cm. Let stand for 10 minutes. Stir, then cover and microwave on HIGH in 2-minute bursts, for 4–6 minutes, stirring once.

Heat the two oils in a large, heavy-based saucepan. Add the ginger, garlic, cardamom, cinnamon and cumin seeds, and sauté over a high heat for 30 seconds, or until aromatic.

Add the prepared vegetables, reserving 10–12 pieces of courgette; stir and sweat over a high heat for 3–5 minutes. Add the sultanas. Pour in the remaining boiling stock, adding extra water if necessary to make a 2-cm depth. Cover and cook for 20 minutes over a medium heat. Uncover the pan and sprinkle in some of the mint leaves. Season with the salt and pepper.

Finely dice the reserved courgette. Check the couscous for hotness, stir in the courgette and transfer to a warmed serving dish. Put the vegetable stew on top. Offer with some harissa as a hot condiment. Diners can squeeze garlic over the vegetables.

To drink: A medium-bodied Merlot or a full-bodied Chenin Blanc.

The wild mushroom season creates much excitement throughout Provence, but especially in the northern reaches of the Var. The mushrooms, which include many boletus varieties, are often packed on pine needles for the trip to market. When buying, check that the caps and stems, when cut open, are worm-free (or relatively so), that the aroma is fresh and sweet and the surface dense, but not damp. This dish takes me back to a happy stay in La Garde Freinet, when we explored markets in the surrounding areas. Visiting Aups on market day, we saw about eight types of wild mushrooms, and local produce celebrated these trophies, using them to stuff pasta, decorate *saucisses* and stud terrines. Everything was excellent, including the *forestière* dishes at every local café and restaurant.

herbed ceps with brandy
cèpes aux herbes, saveur du marc

5–6 large ceps (or else substitute champignons de Paris) about 750 g

4 tablespoons extra virgin olive oil

6 garlic cloves, peeled and sliced

2 shallots, chopped

a handful of fresh oregano, marjoram or flat leaf parsley, or a mixture

120 ml game, chicken or vegetable stock

½ teaspoon dried, crushed chilli flakes (optional)

sea salt flakes and freshly ground black pepper

2 tablespoons cognac or marc de Provence

4 slices of country bread, chargrilled or toasted, or 8 baguette slices, toasted

Serves 4

Use a clean pastry brush (or a fresh pine twig) to brush the mushrooms free of dirt. Twist off the fleshy caps and cut each one in half. Slice the stems into thin rounds, discarding the gritty bases. If small, halve or quarter them instead.

Heat half the olive oil in a heavy-based frying pan. Add the chopped mushroom stems, the garlic, shallots and a little of the herbs, freshly torn. Sauté and stir over a high heat for 3 minutes. Add half the stock, the chilli (if using) and seasoning to taste. Cover and cook for 2 minutes more. Set this mixture aside, but keep warm.

Put the remaining olive oil into a second pan and heat until very hot. Add the halved mushroom caps, toss in more (not all) of the herbs, freshly torn, and stir in the remaining stock. Cook, covered, over a medium heat for 5 minutes, shaking the pan at intervals. Add the reserved mushroom mixture. Shake the pan to combine, or stir gently. Reduce the heat.

Put the cognac into a lightly warmed metal ladle, ignite with a match and carefully pour into the mushroom mixture. When the flames die down, stir and scatter the remaining herbs over the top. Serve on or with the chargrilled bread.

To drink: A weighty, spicy Rioja or a Chianti.

salade des prés (mesclun)
wild meadow salad

On open hillsides, along the edges of pastureland or down in green valleys where streams and waterways run through, it's not unusual, even nowadays, to see intent figures, baskets over their arms, searching for young, succulent wild herb and salad leaves with a concentrated fervour. Mesclun, the famous Niçois leaf salad (its name comes from *mescal*, meaning 'to mix') is said to contain 12 leaf types. Rocket, dandelion, baby lettuce, hyssop, basil and *trévise* (radicchio) are usual; today, *sucrine* (a sweet baby lettuce), oakleaf, chicory, chervil, frisée, escarole and sometimes purslane or lamb's lettuce may also be included in ready-made mixtures.

Wash the salad leaves by hand, then pat dry: a salad spinner is too brutal for this. Put them into a puffed-up plastic bag, seal tightly with a rubber band and chill.

Before serving, crush the garlic against the sides and base of the salad bowl. Toss in the salad leaves and mix gently.

Drizzle the oil over the leaves and toss again (using clean hands is the most satisfactory way). Squeeze over a few drops of lemon juice, if liked, to add sharpness.

To drink: Iced spring water or sparkling mineral water.

4 handfuls of mesclun (1 per person), including pansies or marigolds, if liked

1 large garlic clove, unpeeled

3–4 tablespoons extra virgin olive oil

sea salt flakes and freshly ground black pepper

1 lemon (optional)

Serves 4

asparagus with vinaigrette
asperges en vinaigrette

Although local crops of violet-tipped white asparagus were prized in the past, much plump, green-stalked asparagus is now available from early spring into summer: this is gourmet fare. Even more prized is the thin, slightly tough and curvy wild asparagus, still a local delicacy, but only available in spring. Whichever type you choose, it will respond well to this unusual treatment.

500–650 g green or white or wild asparagus
2 teaspoons coarse salt (gros sel)
1 teaspoon white or black peppercorns
1 shallot, finely diced
2 tablespoons tarragon vinegar or white wine vinegar
a small handful of fresh chervil or chives
6 tablespoons olive oil
1 tablespoon anisette liqueur or pastis

Serves 4

Check the asparagus: either snap off the thick base 5 cm up (where tough meets tender) or peel halfway up the spears and trim 5 cm off the base.

If using wild asparagus, cut them off 20 cm from the tip: the base tends to be very woody.

Heat a large, wide frying pan and fill with boiling water. Add a teaspoon of the salt. Put the asparagus in the water in neatly parallel lines. Return to the boil, then reduce the heat to a simmer and cook for 5–6 minutes for green or wild asparagus, 8–12 minutes for white, depending on size and freshness.

Meanwhile, put the remaining salt, the peppercorns, shallot and half the vinegar into a mortar. Pound for 1–2 minutes with a pestle, then add half the chervil, scissor-chopped. Pound again, adding the remaining vinegar and a little olive oil to create a green paste.

Stir in the remaining olive oil and the anisette. Taste and adjust the seasoning.

Drain the asparagus, but keep it in the pan. Drizzle half the dressing over it and shake to distribute. Do not stir.

Slide the asparagus onto a serving dish. Place the remaining chervil, in a tangle, on the top. Pass the remaining vinaigrette around separately.

To drink: A New World Sauvignon Blanc, a Pinot Gris or water.

Provence-style artichokes with bacon
artichauts provençals aux lardons

Globe artichokes, tiny to immense, from vivid green buds to purple-stippled balls, are an essential feature of the Provençal culinary scene. Locals swear by them as life-enhancing, and claim that indigestion, hangovers and *la grippe* (flu) can be fixed by eating them. Do not be put off by the intricacies of preparation; it is well worth the five minutes of effort because the eating is glorious.

4 large, bell-shaped artichokes
½ lemon
250 g smoked bacon pieces (lardons)
freshly ground black pepper (optional)
freshly grated nutmeg (optional)
100 ml dry white Provençal wine
4 fresh bay leaves
a handful of fresh flat leaf parsley, chopped

Serves 4

Tear off and discard the two tough, outer base layers of leaves from the artichokes. Trim or peel the stems. Slice about 5 cm off the pointed tops of the leaves. Cut each globe in half lengthways.

Use a spoon or a melon baller to dig out the fluffy choke. Discard this and the tiny leaves around it. Rub the lemon over all the cut surfaces. Prepare all the artichokes in the same way.

Heat a large, heavy-based saucepan or flameproof casserole until very hot. Sizzle the lardons until the fat runs: about 3 minutes.

Add some pepper and nutmeg (if using), the wine and bay leaves. Put the artichokes in the pan, cut side down. Cover tightly and cook over a high heat for 5 minutes. Rearrange the artichokes so that the top layer is now at the bottom. Cover and cook over a medium–low heat for 20–25 minutes more. Test the top layer: the artichoke flesh must be easy to pierce with a fork. Continue cooking if necessary. Top up with extra wine if it looks sparse.

Serve the artichokes hot or warm, sprinkled with the luscious reduced sauce and some chopped parsley.

Note: Quarter the artichokes, if necessary, to fit them in the pan.

To drink: A chilled amontillado sherry.

MENTHE
€ 60 6

Provençal herbs, garlic and spices

More than in almost any other country, cooks in France celebrate fresh herbs. Markets are full of succulent cultivated varieties, but huge numbers of herbs also flourish in the wild. Plants gathered from high slopes, *garrigue* (heathland) areas or even the side of the road are particularly prized. Since Provence varies greatly in terrain and culture, herb use is determined by area. (Avoid the aggressively marketed mix known as herbes de Provence. It is far better to dry and mix your own blend.)

Herbs gathered in the wild

Bay (*laurier*). Although cultivated, bay trees self-seed. The leaves scent broths, syrups and brines, and are often combined with other herbs in the classic bouquet garni, useful for flavouring meat, game, poultry and soups.

Wild fennel (*fenouil sauvage*). The pungency of wild fennel far exceeds that of the cultivated variety. In summer the stalks are dried and sold in bunches at fishmongers, market stalls and good supermarkets for stuffing inside fish.

Wild lavender (*lavande sauvage*). The intense, almost medicinal cleanness of lavender can be overpowering. It is used in syrups, pastries and *croquantes,* and sometimes in herbes de Provence.

Wild mint (*nepitella*). Pungent and slightly peppery, this herb (also called catmint) is delicious in salads, herb mixes and with beans.

Oregano (*origan, marjolaine*). This wild form of marjoram has an intoxicating scent when flowering bunches are hung up to dry. Used with other herbs, it excels in tomato-based sauces. (Pot-grown oregano can be bought, but is less intense.)

Rosemary (*romarin*). Growing tall in borders and on rocky hillsides, rosemary bears blue flowers all year round. Whole sprigs, pushed underneath roasting lamb, game, poultry and fish, add a warm, sensual flavour.

Thyme (*thym, farigoule, farigoulette*). The scent of this herb's pale purple blossoms dominates the hillsides. Stocks, sauces, daubes, vinaigrettes, salads and even tisanes use thyme to advantage.

Winter savory (*sarriette de montagne, poivre d'ân, pebre d'ase, pebre d'ai*). This Provençal favourite has white or blue flowers and a stiff, almost prickly appearance. It is often added to cooked broad beans, or wrapped around goats' cheeses, such as Banon.

Cultivated herbs

Basil (*basilic, pistou*). This is the pungent, warmly scented symbolic herb of Provence. Most often on sale is a medium-leafed variety, but large-leaved basils, ornate versions and opal basil (purple), are also common. Soupe au Pistou requires generous quantities of the basil-based sauce called Pistou (page 66). Basil flowers are used in sweet dishes, salads and alcoholic drinks.

Garden celery (*celeri du potager*). This variety of celery (always used in bouquet garni) has thin, hardy stalks and leaves. It releases a pungent scent when handled and has a sharp, refreshing flavour.

Chervil (*cerfeuil*). The feathery fronds of this aniseedy herb are much prized, although it tends to be outranked by fennel and dill.

Chives (*ciboulettes*). Chives enhance chicken, eggs and soft cheeses (but Provençal cooks prefer spring onions or shallot tops).

Hyssop (*hysope*). The bitter, medicinal but lively flavour of hyssop is a delicious addition to drinks.

Lovage (*livèche, ache de montagne*). The long, shaggy leaves release a strong orange and celery aroma when crushed. They add distinction to ravioli fillings, soups and tians.

Flat leaf parsley (*persil commun*). This emerald-leafed, luxuriant herb, excellent both raw and cooked, is extensively used.

Sage (*sauge*). This hardy perennial has strong medicinal overtones with a slightly balsamic edge. It flatters pork and goose.

Sweet marjoram (*marjolaine doux*). Superbly fragrant marjoram has the same uses as oregano, but is sweeter and milder. It is good with vegetables.

Tarragon (*estragon*). This plant, classically used with chervil, parsley and chives, is a *fine herbe*. Useful in vinegars, broths, stuffings and with eggs, tarragon has an intense, elegant flavour.

Minor herbs

Coriander and **fenugreek** are sometimes used in ethnic dishes. **Horseradish** roots and flowers work well with oily fish and game. **Verbena, lemon-scented verbena** and **lemon balm** are frequently used. **Angelica**, sweet and spicy, flatters desserts, as do **scented geranium** leaves and flowers, and **wild violets. Nasturtium** leaves, buds and flowers, and also **hop shoots**, add peppery glamour to salads. **Caper** buds, leaves and flowers, fresh, brined or salted, are an essential flavour of Provençal cooking.

Garlic

Both raw and cooked, garlic is used with abandon in Provence. White garlic (*l'ail blanc*), pearly and smallish, is used for delicate dishes. Pink or purple garlic (*l'ail rose*, locally *l'ail violet*) has a pink-striped, papery outside skin. Bigger and more fiery than the white variety, it goes into dishes that require a generous garlicky boost.

Spices

Provençal favourites include anise seeds, allspice berries, cardamom, cari (curry) mix, coriander, cumin, dill and fennel seeds, dried ginger root, juniper, nutmeg, peppercorns (black, white and green), poppyseeds, pil-pil (a fiery mix), pimiento, ras el hanout (a fragrant mix), saffron, sesame seeds, star anise and vanilla pods.

soupes, fruits de mer et entrées

soups, seafood and lunch dishes

'boiled water' soup
aigo boulido

There is a fairy tale, ancient in origin, that tells of a 'stone soup'. A cook-enchantress, having thrown a stone into the cauldron, encourages other participants to add odds and ends. Eventually, a soup is created. Unappetizing as it may sound, this ancient, frugal soup is a tasty garlic broth that can be easily and quickly made when little food is to hand. When the cupboard is not quite so bare, add whatever you have – perhaps some eggs or fragments of ham or sausage, or maybe a few pieces of leek, some baby peas or beans. This broth is far better than sad packet soups or the bland content of cans. As author Richard Olney suggests, enjoy it as a restorative after 'gastronomic or bacchic excess'.

1.25 litres boiling water
8 garlic cloves, crushed
2 sprigs of fresh sage, bruised
2 sprigs of fresh bay, bruised
2 sprigs of fresh thyme, bruised
1–2 teaspoons rock salt
20 peppercorns
60 ml extra virgin olive oil
8 slices of stale, dry bread, such as baguette
100 g tomme de chèvre (goats' cheese) or Gruyère, sliced (optional)

Serves 4

Heat the water, garlic, herbs, salt, peppercorns and half the olive oil in a large saucepan and boil for 2 minutes. Reduce to a lively simmer and cook, uncovered, for 10–15 minutes longer, crushing the herbs and garlic now and again to release their flavours.

While the soup cooks, toast or chargrill the bread, if you like: this is not traditional, but tastes good. Place two pieces, overlapping, in each soup dish and drizzle the remaining 30 ml oil over them. Add the cheese (if using). (If you prefer, the cheesy croûtes can be served on the side of the dish.)

Ladle the hot broth into the bowl (some people prefer it poured through a sieve) and serve immediately, while steaming hot.

To drink: A rustic red wine from southern France, Italy or Spain.

chestnut-leek chowder
garbure de chataignes et poireaux

Chestnuts and chestnut flour porridge or bread were once survival fare, so many Provençals would prefer to forget them. Now, along with chickpeas and spelt (all ancient foodstuffs of this region), young chefs are reviving interest in them. We were served a soup like this at an *oustalet* (hostelry) in Lourmarin in the Luberon.

24 fresh chestnuts in their shells
1.5 litres hot chicken, pork or vegetable stock
1 leek
2 celery stalks, with leaves, cut in 1-cm slices
1 fresh bouquet garni: bay, thyme and rosemary, tied together
2 tablespoons chestnut flour or chickpea flour
5 tablespoons crème fraîche or thick natural yoghurt, to serve
rock salt and freshly ground black pepper
2 tablespoons extra virgin olive oil

Serves 4–6

Carefully make a 2.5-cm slash in each chestnut shell through to the flesh. Put in a bowl, add 100 ml boiling water and microwave, covered, on HIGH, for 5 minutes. (Alternatively, put into a saucepan and boil for 20–30 minutes.) Let cool slightly, then drain and shell them and discard the inner skin and fibres.

Chop the chestnuts and put into a large saucepan with the hot stock. Add the white parts of the leek, chopped, but reserve a 15-cm length of the green top. Add the celery and bouquet garni, then cover the pan and simmer for 20 minutes, or until tender. Remove the bouquet garni and, in a food processor, process the soup into a thick chowder. Return this to the pan and simmer.

Blend the chestnut flour with 2 tablespoons of the crème fraîche, then stir in 2 tablespoons cold water. Whisk this liaison into the chowder. Continue to cook for 5 minutes, seasoning to taste.

Meanwhile, cut the leek greens in half across the middle and shred them lengthways as finely as possible. Wash and shake dry. Heat the olive oil in a frying pan and sizzle the greens until they are vivid and tender.

Serve the soup with the crème fraîche and leek shreds stirred in.

Note: If no fresh chestnuts can be found, use the vacuum-packed variety, or canned unsweetened chestnuts, whole or puréed.

To drink: A dry oloroso sherry will round out this soup.

This gardener's soup is enriched with pistou – a paste of garlic, basil, cheese and olive oil. Pistou derives its name from the word for 'pestle', the pounding tool from which it is traditionally made. Pesto, the Ligurian equivalent, contains nuts, but none are used in this recipe. In the past, this garden vegetable soup was thick and plain, containing only potatoes, beans, tomatoes and pasta. Today, most Provençal cooks add several kinds of bean, plus courgettes, carrots and onion. Freshly podded coco beans are a favourite ingredient. In their place, you might use fresh or canned white haricot, cannellini or butter beans instead. Fresh or defrosted broad beans could also be substituted. Stir in the glorious pistou at serving time: a sensory overload.

soup with pistou
soupe au pistou

2 litres boiling water

1 fresh bouquet garni: parsley, thyme, celery and bay, tied together

250 g pumpkin, marrow, squash or sweet potato, seeded, peeled and cubed

200 g fresh coco beans or equivalent (see introduction)

2 carrots, sliced

2 onions, sliced

200 g small potatoes, quartered

200 g green beans, such as haricot or runner beans, cut into 10-cm pieces

2 medium courgettes, sliced

a handful of broken spaghetti, vermicelli or short macaroni

2 tomatoes, blanched, peeled and cubed

crusty bread, to serve

Pistou

1 teaspoon rock salt

freshly ground black pepper

6 young garlic cloves, chopped

a handful of fresh basil leaves and basil buds, torn

50 g Parmesan or pecorino cheese, grated

25 g tomme de chèvre (goats' cheese), grated

150 ml extra virgin olive oil

Serves 4–6

Pour the boiling water into a large soup pan. Add the bouquet garni, pumpkin, coco beans, carrots, onions and potatoes, and return to the boil. Reduce the heat to a moderate simmer, then cover and cook for 20 minutes.

Add the green beans, courgettes, pasta and tomatoes. Continue cooking for 10 minutes, until the vegetables and pasta are soft.

Meanwhile, make the pistou. Put the salt, pepper, garlic and basil into a mortar and pound to a paste with a pestle. Add some of the cheese and a splash of the olive oil, and pound until a stiff paste forms. Continue adding the remaining cheese and oil, pounding each addition. The final paste should be thick and rich.

Clean the pestle and place it back in the sauce in the mortar at the centre of the table: a dramatic presentation.

Ladle the soup into big, individual bowls and let diners stir in their own pistou as they eat. Serve with crusty bread.

Note: Pistou can be made in a small food processor. Put all the ingredients, apart from 100 ml of the olive oil, in the bowl and pulse together. With the machine running, add the remaining oil in a steady stream. Do not overprocess.

To drink: A woody Chardonnay or a crisp fruity rosé.

Recent renewed interest in old varieties of grain has given *épautre* or spelt (*Triticum spelta*), a forerunner of today's wheat, a new lease of life. However, if truth be told, spelt, like lentils, barley and chickpeas, has always been a staple foodstuff in the Mediterranean. Look for it in wholefood stores, specialist delis and ethnic grocers, and try to buy from suppliers where turnover is rapid. This hearty farmhouse soup is delicious, and contains *missoun*, a famous Provençal sausage made during the winter. *Andouillette*, an intricate tripe sausage with a rich, earthy flavour, is more widely available and can be used instead. Failing that, a dense, garlicky polony will also work well. Whatever you use, the sausage is always served as a separate course after the soup itself. If preferred, you can serve it for another meal, with some country bread and Dijon mustard.

spelt soup with sausage
soupe épautre au missoun

200 g spelt, soaked for 5–6 hours in boiling water, drained

1.5 litres boiling water

1 missoun, andouillette or dense-textured pork boiling sausage, about 350–400 g

4 tablespoons extra virgin olive oil

4 garlic cloves, chopped

2 onions, thinly sliced

1 head of fennel, thinly sliced, fronds saved for garnish

2 carrots, thinly sliced

4 fresh bay leaves, lightly crushed

30 ml concentrated chicken bouillon

rock salt and freshly ground black pepper

Serves 4–6

Combine the drained spelt and the boiling water in a large saucepan. Return to the boil, bubble for 10 minutes, then skim off any scum. Cover, reduce the heat to a lively simmer and cook for 1½ hours, or until the grain is semi-tender. Add the missoun for the last 20 minutes of this cooking time.

Meanwhile, heat the olive oil in a second pan, add the garlic, onions, fennel, carrots and bay leaves, and sizzle for 5 minutes. Ladle in 350 ml of the soup, followed by the bouillon. Cover, reduce the heat to a gentle simmer and cook for 20–30 minutes.

Once the spelt is bite-tender and crushable (test with the back of a wooden spoon), add the vegetable mixture from the second pan. Cover and cook (still with the sausage) for 10 minutes longer. Remove the sausage, then taste the soup and adjust the seasoning.

Serve the soup at the table, ladling it into big bowls and garnishing with the reserved, chopped fennel fronds.

Note: If spelt is not available, substitute pearl barley or even Camargue red rice.

To drink: Try a chilled beer or a Riesling.

Fish markets in Provence are a fascination and a delight. The shimmering, ocean-fresh creatures caught that morning are invariably sold whole. Buyers smell, prod and inspect every item: they expect the tiny, scuttling *favouille* crabs (charmingly nicknamed *enragées*) to react angrily to their touch. The French approach to food shopping means that markets, such as the pretty one in Saint-Tropez, do a roaring trade. Of all the fish in Provence that give an intense taste of sea freshness, little red mullet, known as 'woodcock of the sea', must be my favourite: the mild, sweet-salt flavour is unique. Very little needs to be done to these pretty fish; in fact, in Provence their liver (and even guts) are sometimes left in, so they are enjoyed in their entirety. In this recipe, they are cleaned and gutted, but the scales are left on. Once salted and cooked, the skin and scales come off together with one swift pull at eating time. This leaves immaculate, flavourful fillets on a central backbone, easy to prise off. Serve with a little *persillade* and you have bliss on a plate!

pan-cooked red mullet
rougets poêlés

8 small or 12 tiny red mullet, livers retained, cleaned but not scaled

2 tablespoons sea salt crystals

4 tablespoons extra virgin olive oil

2 lemons or limes, halved

persillade: 2 garlic cloves and a small handful of parsley, finely chopped (optional)

Serves 4

Dampen the fish, then roll them in the salt crystals to coat them.

Heat two large, non-stick frying pans until very hot. Divide the oil between them and add half the fish to each pan. Sizzle on a high heat for 1½ minutes, using tongs to turn the fish carefully. Cook for another 2 minutes, or until the flesh is set and a delicate white. Slide the fish onto a serving dish or individual dishes.

Encourage diners to use their fingers to pull off and discard the salt-crusted scaly skin. Squeeze some lemon juice over the delicate fillets, and scatter with the persillade, if liked. The delicate fillets can then be eaten with fingers or a fork. (Don't forget the livers: they taste delicious.)

Note: When whole fresh mullet are hard to get, fillets of red mullet (scaled) may be used instead. Cook these similarly, but decrease the salt to a sprinkle and reduce the heat slightly. These can be eaten skin and all.

If no red mullet is available, try to find some small red gurnard or red snapper.

Several kinds of red mullet (some confusingly called 'golden mullet') exist. They may also go under the name of goat fish, *rouget barbet* or *rouget de roche*.

To drink: Chilled Muscadet or Chablis, or even an icy manzanilla sherry.

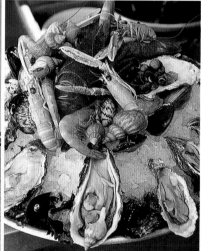

Provençal fish and seafood

Fish and seafood matter more to many Provençals than meat and poultry. Indeed, seafood is one of Provence's claims to fame, and the glorious coastline still produces an amazing 600 varieties of sea creatures. Certainly, there are 'factory ships' far off the coast, but most fishing, strictly governed by EU regulations, is done by long-line or trawlers with approved net sizes. Closer to the shore, pots are used for catching lobsters, crayfish and crabs.

The range of white fish and oily fish on sale – some of it still alive – is astonishing. The smaller and bonier fish that have much scaly waste, or the collection of small mixed seafish sold as *poissons de roche*, are perfect for making the initial stock used for fish soup of several kinds.

Inevitably, there are many great seafood dishes in Provence. One of the best known is *bouillabaisse*, a fish soup-stew. The tradition is to serve its broth first, with croûtes of toasted bread floating on top. On these sit dabs of *rouille* (see page 83) sprinkled with grated Gruyère. Next comes the fish itself, poached in the aromatic broth. To help protect the integrity of this famous dish, there is a 'Charter for Marseilles *bouillabaisse*'. Which other nation would care enough to do this?

Sardines, more often associated with Portugal and Spain, are still a major catch in Provence. Rowdy, festive *sardinades* take place in coastal communities on Sundays.

Other feasts and fast days in Provence centre on another kind of fish – cod, imported from Norway and Iceland. Air-dried salt cod, called *baccala*, and wind-dried but unsalted cod (stockfish), called *stoccafisso* or *estocaficada*, have been staples of the Provençal diet for centuries. Soaked for 24–48 hours, then cooked in the same way as fresh fish, salt cod has a meaty density. It is served as a purée, as fishcakes, covered in batter or in a rich stew, and is essential fare for Christmas Eve's 'Grand Supper'. Unsalted stockfish is an acquired taste: distinctive but alkaline and odd.

If salt cod and dried cod are part of the culture in Provence, so too is the tiny silver fish called the anchovy, which has been popular in the region since Roman times. The anchovy has the same sort of significance in Provençal cooking that fish sauces have in Asian cooking, and the rationale is very similar. Layered and salted whole in barrels, or filleted, brined or salted, then canned or bottled, the anchovy develops an intense savouriness. Many are used to make pissalat (see page 146), an intense, dry paste used as a spiced condiment on pissaladière and pizza, or with lemon juice, garlic and oil as a dipping sauce.

Larger fish, often cooked whole, are chargrilled, sautéed or deep-fried. Others are cooked *en papillotte* (wrapped in paper). A few will be poached and baked, but most are served simply with olive oil, fresh herbs and some citrus or tomato sauces rather than complex reduction sauces or cream- and butter-based ones.

Mediterranean red mullet have a most distinctive salt-sweet taste of the sea. Similar-looking, although very different, fish are red snapper and red gurnard, which you can substitute.

Bream of different types – particularly gilt-head bream – John Dory, conger eels, whiting and hake are all enjoyed. Lotte, also called angler-fish or monkfish, is a trophy; and a large, dense-fleshed *loup de mer* or sea bass is cherished. Tuna and swordfish, major 'game' fish, are often sold from the jetty.

A *plateau de fruits de mer* provides a selection of whatever is caught that day or available at the market. Many shellfish, even mussels and clams, are eaten uncooked and live, much to the consternation of some tourists. When cooked, mussels, small clams, such as *praires* and *tellines*, and the big Venus clams are often prepared with a little wild fennel or dill. Some of these shellfish may become the basis of a risotto or a sauce for spaghetti. Squid, called *encornets* or *calamars*, like octopus (*poulpe*), is much enjoyed raw, or fried in sautés or added to stews and soups.

Glorious, iodine-tasting oysters are available all year round. They can be *plats* (flat shells) or *creuses* (cupped shells), and many different types are available. Colours, flesh types, textures and flavours vary hugely. Size is determined by age. Often, long 'refining' in the *claires* (pools) leads to plump, large oysters known as *fines de claires*. Only rarely are oysters cooked.

Sought-after specialities in Provence include *oursins* (sea urchins) still in their black prickly shells, and *violets* (barnacle-like shellfish). A luxury item to try is *poutargue*, or 'Provençal caviar' (see page 27). This historical fish product is the washed, salted and pressed egg sacs of the grey mullet, compacted into a block 1 cm thick and sealed by being dipped in wax. You cut the blocks into thin slices, remove the wax and enjoy the roe.

Provence boasts crustaceans of all sizes, colours and varieties, many of them with thrilling names: *crevettes gris*, *crevettes roses* or *bouquets*, *amethystes*, *corails*, *gambas*, *tigres* or even *bananes* are typical. Look for local langoustes (spiny lobsters without claws), the rare, more delicate, flat, shovel-nosed local slipper lobsters called *cigales* and freshwater crayfish.

Fish from rivers and lakes, which include carp, tench, perch and trout, are keenly prized. Sea trout and salmon are also in demand, especially by younger cooks. Some fish is farmed.

Flat fish, less in demand than in the past, are usually pan-fried. Sashimi and sushi, introduced for Japanese tourists, are at present surprisingly popular.

When you eat seafood in Provence, some crisp white wine is de rigueur.

Carpaccio is the name of an Italian painter of the Renaissance who loved to paint using red pigments. The term has been adopted as relevant for raw wafers of beef and loin of tuna, which is also scarlet. Try to buy line-caught tuna fresh from the wharf, where their glossy, torpedo-shaped bodies are lined up for sale. We saw such a sight in Le Lavandou. Make and eat this dish *à la minute* (within minutes); although the lemon helps to keep it fresh, it rapidly loses its appealing colour if left sitting. It makes a delicious snack or meal.

tuna carpaccio with capers
carpaccio du thon aux câpres

500 g fresh tuna loin, sliced into 4 or 6 pieces (ideally by the fishmonger)

8 tablespoons extra virgin olive oil

4 lemons or 8 limes

75 g salted capers, rinsed and chopped

freshly ground black pepper

1 teaspoon anchovy paste (page 146)

fresh nasturtium leaves, caper leaves or rocket (optional) and 12 caper berries, to garnish

Serves 4

Ensure that the tuna is chilled, then place each piece between two sheets of greaseproof paper. Using a rolling pin, roll and flatten each piece until it's the size of a dinner plate.

Pour a tablespoon of the olive oil into each of four dinner plates. Tilt them so that the oil covers the whole surface.

Gently transfer each slice of tuna to an oiled plate (inverting it is the easiest method). Squeeze one of the lemons and brush the juice all over the fish. Let stand while the dressing is made: about 5 minutes, no longer.

Put the remaining oil, the juice of two more lemons, the capers, pepper and anchovy paste into a food processor. Pulse in brief bursts until chopped, not puréed. Pour into a serving bowl.

Grind some pepper over the tuna. Cut the remaining lemon into wedges and use to garnish the plates, along with the nasturtium leaves (if using) and the caper berries. Drizzle a circle of dressing over each plate.

Serve without delay, offering fougasse, baguette or other crusty bread as an accompaniment.

Note: If necessary, the flattened tuna and dressing can be prepared in advance, but the lemon juice should not be brushed over the fish until the last minute.

To drink: A flinty white wine, such as Pouilly-Fumé, or a zesty Sauvignon Blanc from New Zealand, South Africa or Chile, or an Australian Riesling.

sardines stuffed with spinach
sardines farcies aux épinards

This unusual but beautiful dish exists in slightly different forms all around the Mediterranean. In Sardinia, for example, the stuffing contains nuts and dried currants. This recipe uses some of Provence's famed crystallized fruits (clementines, lemons or mandarins) – not traditional, but delicious nonetheless – or, if you like, you could use candied peel. In times past, sweet foodstuffs, particularly in Arab-influenced dishes such as this one, were indicators of wealth and plenty. Try this fascinating combination of tastes for yourself.

24 small, fresh sardines, beheaded, cleaned and scaled

6 tablespoons extra virgin olive oil

600 g fresh spinach or Swiss chard tops, rinsed, not shaken dry and chopped

6 spring onions, chopped

4 garlic cloves, chopped

4 tablespoons finely chopped fresh parsley

1 teaspoon sea salt flakes

½ teaspoon freshly grated nutmeg

2 hard-boiled eggs, chopped

75 g fresh breadcrumbs or pain d'épice (spice cake) crumbs

75 g Provençal crystallized fruits or candied peel, sliced

a small handful of fresh mint, scissor-snipped, or 12 whole mint leaves, to garnish

Serves 4–6

Put the sardines on a board and flatten them out, skin side down, by pressing with your fingertips. Pull up and free the central spine at the head end, then snip it off near the tail. Lift out, and the rib bones should come with it.

To make the stuffing, heat half the olive oil in a frying pan. When hot, add all the spinach, spring onions, garlic and parsley, bring to a high heat, then reduce the heat, cover and cook for 2 minutes. Stir well, then let cool, uncovered.

Spread half the spinach mixture into a large, ovenproof dish. To the other half add the salt, nutmeg, eggs and breadcrumbs. Stir in half the crystallized fruits. Spoon this stuffing onto the flattened fish fillets at the widest end. Roll up neatly with the tail on the outside.

Preheat the oven to 220°C (425°F) Gas 7.

Arrange the stuffed sardines in rows on top of the spinach mixture in the dish, leaving the tails up or down. Scatter the remaining crystallized fruits over all, and drizzle with the remaining 3 tablespoons olive oil.

Bake towards the top of the oven for 20–25 minutes, or until the fish are fragrant and tender. Serve hot, cool or cold, garnished with the fresh mint.

To drink: Chenin Blanc, ideally from the Loire, or an off-dry Vouvray.

sprats crisp-fried with lemon
friture de nonats de Nice

grapeseed oil and virgin olive oil, for frying
1 kg tiny sprats or whitebait
250 g plain flour, for coating
1 teaspoon cayenne pepper
1 teaspoon fine salt

To serve
100 g Anchoïade (page 16)
a handful of flat leaf or curly parsley, chopped
2 lemons, cut into wedges
50 g caper berries (optional)

Serves 4–6

The tiny young of seafish, known as 'fry' in English (*friture* or *nonats* in French), are often on sale in blue, plastic-lined boxes at the fish market in Vieux Nice and in other ports around Provence. These are destined for rolling in seasoned flour, followed by simple frying. For prettier presentation, they can be pressed into rings before frying (see method).

Pour a 50:50 mixture of the two oils into a heavy-based frying pan, making a depth of 2 cm. Heat to 185–190°C (365–375°F), or until a cube of bread browns in 10 seconds.

Wash the fish and drain in a colander. Mix the flour, cayenne and salt, and sift some onto a sheet of greaseproof paper on a board. Put 2 handfuls of fish on the flour and shape into a ring. Sprinkle with more seasoned flour and press down firmly with a fish slice or potato masher. Slide the ring into the hot oil and cook until crisp: about 2 or 3 minutes. Lift out and keep hot while you cook the remaining fish.

Serve with a little bowl of anchoïade in the centre of the ring, a scattering of parsley, some lemon wedges and caper berries dotted around the plate, if you like

To drink: A crisp, fragrant white Bellet, aged Riesling, aged Chardonnay, or another white Burgundy.

clams sautéed with fennel
tellines poêlés au fenouil

Wild fennel grows with abandon in Provence, and its intense aniseed flavour is perfect with all types of clam – the liveliest your fish market is offering.

Shake the clams in a colander under cold running water for a minute or so. Let drain.

Slice the fennel crossways into ovals, then cut into match-sized strips. Pile into a dish containing half the lemon juice, stirring to coat them.

Heat the butter and olive oil in large frying pan. Add the drained fennel, the garlic, chilli (if using) and fennel seeds and cook over a high heat for 2 minutes. Pour in the clams and mix well. Cover the pan, shake once or twice, then reduce the heat to medium. Cook for 2–4 minutes, or until all the clams are opened. (Discard any that remain closed.)

Uncover the pan, increase the heat and stir. Add the pastis and enough of the remaining lemon juice to balance the flavours. Season to taste.

Serve hot in bowls with lemon wedges and chunks of country bread for soaking up the delicious juices.

To drink: A young Chardonnay or Pinot Gris such as one from Alsace.

1 kg small live clams, such as tellines
½ head of fennel
freshly squeezed juice of 2 lemons
25 g salted butter
2 tablespoons extra virgin olive oil
2 garlic cloves, finely chopped
1 dried, hot red chilli, seeded and crumbled (optional)
1 teaspoon fennel seeds, preferably wild
1 tablespoon pastis or similar aniseed liqueur
sea salt flakes and freshly ground black pepper
lemon wedges
crusty bread

Serves 4–6

salt cod in piquant sauce
morue en raïto

The origins of *raïto* (or *rayto*), a classic Christmas Eve dish all over the northern Var, are lost in the mists of time. Maybe it came to Marseilles with Phocaean sailors. Who knows? But it's clear that salt cod (*morue* or *merlussa* in Niçois) and stockfish (wind-dried cod) have been imported from Scandinavia for millennia.

900g–1 kg salt cod or stockfish (middle piece) or 3 x 400-g packs presoaked '12-hour process' salt cod

100 g plain white flour

75–100 ml virgin olive oil, for frying

a small handful of fresh flat leaf parsley, scissor-snipped (optional)

Raïto

3 tablespoons extra virgin olive oil

2 onions, thinly sliced

300 ml young, tannic red wine, such as Gigondas

350 g fresh tomatoes, blanched, peeled and chopped, or equivalent canned version

1 fresh bouquet garni: orange zest, celery, dried fennel twigs, parsley and rosemary, tied together

1 teaspoon sea salt

1 teaspoon crushed black peppercorns

100 g salt-cured black olives, plus extra to garnish

30 g salted capers, plus extra to garnish

rosemary sprigs, to garnish

Serves 6

If using ready-prepared salt cod, no soaking will be required. If using classic dry salt cod, cover it with at least 7.5 cm cold water in a non-metallic bowl. Cover and refrigerate for 24 hours, changing the water every 6 hours. The cod will whiten and plump up. Drain and pat dry on kitchen paper. Cut into 20 pieces, removing as many bones as possible.

To make the raïto, heat the olive oil in a heavy-based saucepan and fry the onions until softened and golden: about 10 minutes. Stir in the wine, 250 ml water, the tomatoes, bouquet garni, salt and peppercorns. Cook, stirring frequently, for about 40 minutes, or until thickened and reduced.

Take 2 tablespoons of the flour and mix to a paste with 6 tablespoons cold water. Stir this into the raïto. Cook, stirring, for 10 minutes more. Remove the bouquet, then transfer the sauce to a food processor and whizz until smooth. Stir in the olives and capers, then set aside. Preheat the oven to 200°C (400°F) Gas 6.

Put the remaining flour on a plate and coat the cod portions in it. Heat the oil for frying until very hot. Fry the cod for 2 minutes on each side, until golden. Drain. Spoon half the raïto into a large baking dish or casserole. Put the fish on top. Spoon the remaining sauce over. Bake for 15–25 minutes, until very hot. Garnish with olives, capers, rosemary and parsley.

To drink: A weighty Gigondas, a classic claret or a Shiraz.

salt cod purée
brandade de morue

Brandade, it is said, comes from the verb *brandir* or *branler*, which means 'to swing', an allusion to the wide movements the spoon makes when beating this rich, creamy purée. Nîmes, in the Camargue, was once renowned for its stockfish *brandade*: maybe the recipe originated there. Some variations include walnut oil, others sliced truffles. This well-loved dish is often made using salt cod and potatoes, the latter a more recent addition. This purée is usually eaten hot, scooped onto thin toasts, or put into tiny vol-au-vent cases. Once eaten during periods of fasting, *brandade* is now much enjoyed each Christmas Eve in Provence, and during other times when meat is not supposed to be eaten.

550 g salt cod, soaked and drained as described on page 80
1 sprig each of fresh thyme, fresh bay and parsley
4 garlic cloves, crushed, peeled and chopped
90 ml extra virgin olive oil, plus extra if needed
120 ml creamy milk, heated to near-boiling
400 g hot, freshly boiled potatoes
freshly grated nutmeg
sea salt flakes and freshly ground pepper
half a cucumber, sliced, and black olives (optional) to garnish
24–32 thin slices of baguette, toasted or oven-dried, to serve

Serves 4 (or 8 as an appetizer)

Put the cod, the herbs and enough water to cover into a medium, heavy-based saucepan. Bring to the boil.

Reduce the heat to a simmer, cover the pan and cook for 30–35 minutes, or until flaky and very tender. Drain in a sieve.

Discard all the fish bones, but retain the skin: its gelatinous nature helps the emulsion. Break up the cod into smallish pieces.

Return the fish to the pan, put over a medium heat and add the garlic, 1 tablespoon of the olive oil and 2 tablespoons of the milk. Beat together with a heavy wooden spoon or a potato masher, using a circular movement in one direction.

Add more oil and hot milk (not all of it), and beat until the mixture is creamy.

Now add the hot potatoes, broken up with a fork. Mash and pound, still over a medium heat, to incorporate them into the mixture.

Add the remaining oil and hot milk over the heat until a creamy purée results. Taste and season with salt, pepper and nutmeg.

Divide the purée between 4 large (or 8 small) serving plates and surround it with thinly sliced cucumber and black olives (if using). Serve with hot toasts.

To drink: A pastis or crisp southern Rhône rosé.

This magnificent dish, not so much a soup as an entire meal, is one of the most hotly disputed dishes ever created. The contradictions that exist, all over Provence and elsewhere, make cooking it almost a comedy. In Marseilles, cooks declare that without *rascasse* (scorpion fish), it is a fake; with lobster (as in Paris), it is a travesty; adding mussels and potatoes (as in Toulon) is incorrect; including tiny cuttlefish (popular in Martigues) is abhorrent. Essentially, true bouillabaisse is a tasty fish broth made from tiny rockfish, or the carcasses and trimmings of cod, snapper, whiting and unimportant smaller fish. To these must be added garlic, onion, tomatoes, herbs, saffron and seasoning. Once cooked, the mixture is pressed into a sieve and the solids discarded. Next, the more substantial fish varieties, such as scorpion fish, monkfish, John Dory, bream and eel, are left whole and poached in this liquid. The manner of serving is in stages: into each dish go several dry croûtes, a dollop of *rouille* (a spicy red sauce) and some Gruyère, then the broth is poured into the dish. This is enjoyed first. After that the fish itself is served.

Provençal fish soup with 'rust' sauce
bouillabaisse et sa rouille

50 ml extra virgin olive oil

4 garlic cloves, chopped

2 onions, sliced

6 tomatoes, chopped

1 large fresh bouquet garni: orange zest, parsley, thyme, celery and fennel, tied together

450 g small rockfish or the carcasses (without gills) of cod, whiting, etc.

200 ml dry white wine

2 pinches of saffron

1 teaspoon sea salt crystals

½ teaspoon dried red pepper flakes (optional)

Fish

1 scorpion fish or red gurnard, cut in 2-cm slices

1 x 12-cm piece prepared monkfish, cut in 2-cm slices

1 x 12-cm piece John Dory or bream, cut in 2-cm slices

1 x 12-cm piece red snapper, in 2-cm slices

4 small red mullet or 1 large, in 2-cm slices

2 tablespoons pastis (optional)

other additions, such as tiny crabs (optional)

To serve

24 croûtes

200 ml rouille

100 g Gruyère cheese, grated

Serves 4–6

Heat the oil in a heavy-based saucepan or flameproof casserole and sauté the garlic and onions over a high heat for 2 minutes. Add the tomatoes, bouquet garni and the rockfish. Cook hard for 3 more minutes. Pour in 1.5 litres cold water and the wine, and bring back to the boil. Skim off any scum, then boil hard for 8–10 minutes, pressing down on the fish to extract all their flavours.

Meanwhile, using a pestle and mortar, pound together the saffron, salt and red pepper flakes (if using). Stir half the mixture into the soup, turn off the heat and let stand for 5 minutes more.

Ladle and/or pour the pan contents into a colander or large sieve set over a bowl. Press down hard to extract all the juices and flavours but do not mash. Discard these solids, but reserve the bouquet garni.

Return the soup to its original saucepan. Add the five fish types in the order listed in the ingredients, leaving the more delicate ones until last: these will sit on top.

Sprinkle over the remaining saffron mixture and add the reserved bouquet garni. Bring the pan contents to a gentle boil and cook for 2 minutes. Reduce the heat to a lively simmer, then part-cover and cook for 5–8 minutes more, or until all the fish is tender and very hot. Taste the liquid and adjust the seasoning, if necessary: it should be a spicy reddish broth.

Add several croûtes, each with a spoonful of rouille (see below) on top, and a sprinkle of Gruyère. To serve the broth, ladle it into individual dishes.

Serve the fish after the broth, offering any remaining croûtes, rouille and cheese with it.

To make rouille: Dip a 5-cm baguette into the fish broth. Squeeze it dry. Pound it with a similar volume of Aïoli (see page 15) and 2 pinches each of chilli flakes and pimiento (or 1 tablespoon of harissa).

To drink: Bandol rosé, a Chablis or a Bellet, or dry white wine from Cassis.

Provençal fish soup with aïoli
bourride

Fish soups are a speciality of coastal Provence; many, like *bourride*, are world famous. In Sète, this version, which uses four or five fish varieties, is particularly appreciated. The fish broth is enriched, flavoured and thickened with garlicky *aïoli*; more *aïoli* is spread on the croûtes served in it. This grand dish is unusual in containing egg yolks and thick cream as additional enrichments, so needs little to follow it – perhaps a few scented grapes or some melon, a sliver of blue cheese and a small, intense black coffee to finish.

800 g assorted firm-fleshed white fish, such as turbot, sea bass, sea bream, monkfish and grey mullet or whiting, cleaned and cut into 2-cm slices

4 slices of fresh lemon (plus a 30-cm sliver of zest to garnish)

2 onions, sliced

1 fresh bouquet garni: thyme, parsley, bay and fennel, tied together

4 garlic cloves, peeled and chopped

1 teaspoon sea salt crystals

16 white peppercorns, lightly crushed

4 medium potatoes, quartered, trimmed and peeled

300 ml medium-dry white wine

60 ml crème fraîche

3 large, free-range egg yolks

250 ml Aïoli (page 15)

toasted baguette, to serve

extra fresh herbs, to garnish (optional)

Serves 4–6

Rinse the cleaned fish in a colander, discarding all debris, such as gills and scales.

Put the lemon slices, onions and bouquet garni into a large, heavy-based saucepan or flameproof casserole. Scatter in the garlic, salt and peppercorns. Put the potatoes on top and pour over 1 litre water and the wine. Bring to the boil, then reduce the heat to a brisk simmer and cook, uncovered, for 10 minutes. Remove the potatoes with a slotted spoon and set aside.

Add all the fish to the broth. Replace the potatoes on top and return to a simmer. Cover the pan and cook for 10–12 minutes, or until all the fish is flaky and the potatoes are cooked, but still whole.

Using a fish slice or skimmer, transfer the fish and potatoes to a large, heatproof serving dish or casserole.

Strain the stock into a measuring jug and discard the solids. If there is more than 800 ml, boil it, uncovered, until it reduces to this amount. Return it to the measuring jug.

Into the same hot saucepan used for the fish, put the crème fraîche, egg yolks and two-thirds of the aïoli. Whisk together quickly, then pour in half the hot stock. Whisk again.

Cook over a medium heat, never letting the mixture boil, for 3–4 minutes, stirring or whisking constantly to achieve a velvety soup. Add the remaining stock, then keep at a very gentle simmer. Taste and adjust the seasoning.

Ladle about a quarter of the finished broth over the fish. Garnish with the sliver of zest and fresh herbs if liked. Keep hot.

Ladle the remainder of the broth into soup dishes. Add several croûtes, each with a teaspoonful of the reserved aïoli on top. Eat this first, and follow with the fish and potatoes.

Note: Two pinches of powdered saffron may be added to the thickened broth for extra flavour and colour.

To drink: A substantial wine, such as a Blanc de Blancs de Cassis AOC, would be an excellent match; so would a Grand Cru Riesling from Alsace or Austria, or a New World Riesling.

Sea bass is considered a splendid fish, and Provençal methods of cooking it are simple but very stylish. Since fennel grows wild in many coastal places, and dried twigs and seed heads can be bought at most supermarkets, it is often used to add its distinctive flavour to seafood. If you can't get hold of any, use rosemary, bay or thyme twigs instead, but double the amount of fennel seeds used. The herb twigs are sometimes flambéed for dramatic effect and flavour at the end of cooking time. Locals might use *branda* for this, a local *marc de Provence*, but any sort of spicy *eau de vie* or even cognac could be used instead. Besides chunky lemon wedges, you might also accompany this dish with Anchoïade, Aïoli, Rouille or Pistou (pages 16, 15, 83 and 66).

sea bass grilled over dried fennel twigs
loup de mer au fenouil

1.5–2 kg sea bass, cleaned and scaled

2 handfuls of dried fennel twigs, plus feathery seed heads, or dried celery or thyme twigs

1 teaspoon sea salt crystals

1–2 teaspoons fennel seeds (preferably wild), dill seeds or anise seeds

20 black or white peppercorns

60 ml extra virgin olive oil

2 tablespoons marc de Provence, branda, eau de vie or cognac

1 lemon, cut into wedges

crusty bread, to serve

a large hinged metal grill, with handles

Serves 4–6

If using a barbecue, light the charcoal and let it burn down to embers. You want a slow, steady heat from it.

Pat the fish dry inside and out. Make 3 parallel, 1-cm slashes in each side. Push a herb twig into each slash, and a few more into the head and behind the gills.

Using a pestle and mortar, grind the salt, fennel seeds and peppercorns to a gritty powder. Rub half inside the gut cavity of the fish. Push some herb twigs inside, then put the fish on a large platter, drizzle with some of the olive oil and turn once to coat. Drain, then rub the remaining seasoning into the slashes and all over the skin.

Put the fish on the metal grill at right angles to the handles. Close the top and secure the handles if using a double fish grill.

Place the grill over the embers, or under a grill that has been preheated for at least 8–10 minutes. In the latter case, the fish should sit about 7.5 cm below the grill with an empty pan beneath. Grill the fish for 8 minutes or so.

Brush the fish with olive oil, turn it, brush again and grill for a further 8 minutes, or until cooked through to the bone. The flesh should be white and flaky.

Using 2 fish slices, transfer the fish to a large, heatproof platter and pour any remaining oil over it.

Put the alcohol into a metal ladle, lightly warmed. Carefully set it alight, then pour over the fish: the herbs will char slightly. As the flames die down, squeeze over some lemon juice to douse them completely.

Serve chunks of the hot fish with crusty bread and extra lemon wedges, if liked.

To drink: A Premier Cru Chablis, a Pouilly-Fumé, a Savatiano or a minerally white wine from Greece.

'*Bouquets*' says the label at the Cannes fish market: confusingly, this is the local name for medium-sized prawns, fast-cooked, cooled and packed onto ice. *Crevettes grises*, semi-transparent shrimps jumping with life, are, apart from scuttling crabs and lobsters, the only type sold in this state. Chunky *gambas*, a hand-span long, raw but not live, make silvery-blue ranks. Larger, farmed blue prawns, almost shockingly big, are labelled *tigres*. Smallish, flat *cigales* or slipper lobsters are very rare these days, but small crabs, from long-legged *araignées de mer* (spider crabs) to *favouilles* (shore crabs) are common and popular. Use a selection of whatever is freshest and best at the fishmonger's. This feisty dish, with garlic, ginger, chilli and some spicy hot paste to flatter its taste of the sea, needs clean fingers, large napkins and lots of enthusiastic appetites.

mixed seafood and shellfish sauté
méli-mélo de crustacées

500 g uncooked small or medium prawns in the shell

4 uncooked langoustines or large prawns

4 uncooked small shore crabs (favouilles) or spider crabs (araignées)

4 large live clams

3 tablespoons extra virgin olive oil

2 shallots or 1 small onion, sliced

4 garlic cloves, sliced

2.5-cm piece of fresh ginger, thinly sliced

1 medium-hot green or red chilli, seeded and membranes discarded

1 tablespoon harissa paste

1 teaspoon fennel seeds or dill seeds, lightly crushed

½ teaspoon sea salt flakes

1 red sweet pepper, seeded and cut into strips

250 ml medium-dry Provençal rosé wine

To serve

lemon or lime halves

rye bread and/or crusty ficelle bread

Serves 4

Rinse and scrub all the seafood to ensure that it's free of grit and mud.

Heat the olive oil in a large, heavy frying pan or wok and sauté the shallots and garlic for 2 minutes, stirring occasionally.

Cut the ginger slices into fine shreds, add to the pan along with the chilli, harissa, fennel seeds and salt, and cook for 1 minute, stirring.

Now add the prawns, langoustines, crabs and strips of pepper. Tuck the bodies well into the spicy mixture.

Pour in the wine and cover the pan, then reduce the heat to medium and cook for 4–5 minutes. Stir and reposition the seafood using tongs. Add the clams. Part-cover the pan again and cook for 2 minutes longer, or until the liquid is reduced and the seafood is firm-fleshed and aromatic. Do not overcook.

Serve plain in bowls, accompanied by lemon halves and bread. Alternatively, serve on a bed of freshly cooked spaghetti or vermicelli, tossed quickly in olive oil, garlic and some chopped dill or parsley.

Note: Although some cooks slit the back of raw crustaceans to remove the black vein, it is easy for diners to do this when eating them at the table.

To drink: An off-dry Riesling or a Tokaji, or Pinot Gris from Alsace.

'dog' ravioli
merda di can

Freshly made pasta with fillings relevant to the area are popular throughout Provence, though with none of the range and intricacy of those found in Italy. The most common filling is chard, but pumpkin, meat from the *daube* and walnut, cheese and herb mixtures are also typical. These curious little ravioli are uneven and twisty in shape, accounting perhaps for their local name, which means 'dog shit'. This recipe is a free adaptation of the original. Eat it with a little olive oil or some juices from a *daube* or casserole, or with melted butter and some grated Gruyère. You could also serve with some lightly cooked chard.

Put both the flours into a food processor. Whizz twice to aerate. In a bowl, whisk together the salt, eggs and oil with a fork. With the machine running, add the egg mixture in a steady stream, until the dough clumps together into a ball. Remove, dust with flour and knead briefly until smooth. Wrap in clingfilm and chill for 20 minutes.

To make the filling, put the lardons in a frying pan and cook over a high heat until the fat runs. Add the minced meat and cook, stirring, over a high heat for 3 minutes. Add the garlic, herbs, candied fruit, allspice and 2 tablespoons water. Cook for a further minute.

Cut the chilled pasta dough into 3 equal pieces. Shape into ovals. Wrap 2 pieces in clingfilm and set aside. Roll out the third piece of dough by passing it through a pasta machine, set on the widest setting, number 6. Continue rolling several times more, then fold the pasta in half into a long envelope. Put this through the rollers 3 times.

Change the machine to a narrower setting, and continue rolling until the pasta has reached nearly 1 metre in length. Remove and hang the pasta sheet over a cloth-covered chair to part-dry. Repeat this whole process with the 2 remaining pieces of dough.

To make the ravioli, cut the first sheet of pasta in half crossways. Put one half on a lightly floured work surface.

Take one-third of the filling and put 16 dots of it at regular intervals over 1 half sheet. Use the egg-and-water mixture to brush straight lines between the piles. They should criss-cross each at right angles. Place the second half sheet of pasta on top, and press firmly along the lines of egg wash to seal.

Cut between the pasta pockets to make individual squares. Take 1 square, brush some egg wash on one corner, then fold diagonally to the corner opposite and press to seal. Put on a floured cloth to air-dry for 2 hours. Prepare the rest of the ravioli in the same way.

Cook the pasta in batches of 12 or so in a large saucepan of boiling salted water for about 2 minutes, or until they float. Turn them over and cook for a further minute.

Serve drizzled with some walnut or olive oil. Wetted Swiss chard shreds can be briefly sautéed in the oil first, if liked.

To drink: Try an AOC Bordeaux, a red Bellet or a Chianti.

250 g plain white flour

100 g rye, spelt or buckwheat flour, sifted

½ teaspoon salt

3 large eggs

1 tablespoon walnut oil or extra virgin olive oil, plus extra to serve

1 egg, beaten with 2 tablespoons water

Swiss chard shreds, lightly sautéed, to garnish (optional)

Filling

75 g smoked bacon lardons

100 g minced beef, veal or lamb, or 100 g Swiss chard, washed and chopped

3 garlic cloves, chopped

a handful of fresh herbs: tarragon, basil, mint, parsley or a mixture

2 teaspoons candied or crystallized citrus fruit, chopped

½ teaspoon ground allspice

Serves 4–6 (48 ravioli)

volailles, viandes et gibiers

poultry, meat and game

Provençal meat, game and poultry

The Provençal appetite for intense flavours, wild foods from forests, mountains and marshlands, and many seasonal specialities and rare breeds mean that some splendid meat dishes have been developed here. While seafood is favoured along the coast, more meat is consumed by people living inland. In the Bouches du Rhône, the Carmarguais hold a number of *ferias* (festivals) at which meat-eating is a priority: the black bulls, white horses and horsemen of this area have become legendary, as have their rituals.

Lamb is the most important meat of Provence, and is something of a staple food. The best-known lamb, *agneau de Sisteron*, is produced under strict EU regulations and is identified by an official mark. Raised from three traditional breeds of sheep (and their crosses) – *Merinos d'Arles*, *Préalpes du Sud* and *Mourerous* – the lambs are weaned at 60 days old, then taken to graze on the herb-dotted hillsides in clearly defined (by law) parts of Provence. The lambs are slaughtered at 70–150 days old, and yield a light pink, fine-textured carcass weighing about 13–19 kg. Generations of careful breeding, traditional husbandry and quality grazing result in a delicious meat. A leg of this lamb, roasted very simply with garlic or herbs, and served with flageolets, is magnificent.

Considerable numbers of cattle are raised in the Camargue, where the *Bouvine*, with dark coat and lyre-shaped horns, is the most common breed. These beasts, often reaching 450 kg, are kept exclusively for the *course camarguaise* – bull running and bullfights – and for folk festivals, such as *abrivados*. These mark the arrival of the bulls into towns driven by men on horseback. The *enciero*, when the bulls run loose into towns, creates wild excitement. The bullfights that follow are briefer and less violent than those in Spain. When these *Bouvine* bulls reach 15 years old, they are returned to the herd and eventually buried, horns upwards, facing the sea.

The Camargue breeds another type of bull called *Brave*. Mainly black, with low, forward-tilted horns and weighing up to 650 kg, *Braves* are strong, aggressive and bred for fighting. Most die in the bullring, but their meat is never wasted. Many people believe that such an end is more noble than a trip to the abattoir.

Beef is most famously used in rich, full-flavoured Provençal *daubes* (braises containing wine). A *daube* can be served hot, or cold and jellied. *Daubières*, the traditional earthenware pots in which they are made, are often passed down in families.

Provence is not generally known for its veal, but what there is is of good quality. It is often served as a *blanquette* (white stew) or with a typical local stuffing.

Pork in all its forms is widely enjoyed. It may be grilled, sautéed, braised or roasted; used in sausages, terrines and pâtés; cured as bacon or ham; and made into splendid charcuterie. It also goes into Provence's renowned beef and lamb *daubes*, to which it adds a distinctive depth of flavour. To my mind, pork reaches greatness as *saucisson sec* – a thin, dry-cured sausage that is sold tied in bundles, or as *saucisson d'Arles* – a plump sausage flavoured with donkey meat. These are outstandingly delicious.

In autumn, wild boar (*sanglier*) is hunted. This has rich, dark meat, which is distinctly gamey. However, many people prefer the young boar called *marcassin*, which is cooked like lamb and much more tender.

Deer is another target of the hunt. Venison, cooked with herbs, juniper, allspice or nutmeg, and finished with aromatic wine or fruit sauces, is a treat.

The scrubby landscape of Provence is a good place to rear goats, and their meat is very popular, particularly at Easter. Young goat or kid, spit-roasted with fresh herbs, is a classic dish.

Wild rabbits, as well as hutch-reared ones, are everyday fare in Provence, and there are a multitude of recipes for them. Wild hares, on the other hand, are generally eaten only in the autumn.

Poulterers stock mainly whole chickens, often with head and feet still attached so that purchasers can evaluate the whole bird. Farmyard chickens (*poulardes*) predominate, but there are always some boiling fowl and roasting birds available. During the spring, poussins and demi-poussins are on offer. Many French chickens are named breeds or specifically reared with their own denominations, such as Label Rouge, a guarantee of quality.

Farmed duck and goose are enjoyed particularly in autumn and winter. Duck breasts (*magrets*), often sold in packs, may be cured or smoked. Legs are usually sold raw. Jars of duck confit are also very popular.

Turkey is a low-fat alternative to pork, used in quickly cooked sautées and blanquettes.

Game birds of all kinds, in season, are trussed and barded with great artistry. Partridge, pheasant, guinea fowl, squab pigeons and quail are just some of the indigenous creatures that represent the wild heart of Provence, though some of these are now farmed.

In a region that has in the past known famine, there is a frugality in the people's approach to meat: nothing is wasted. As a result, many types of offal are eaten, and there are many recipes that are not for the squeamish. One popular dish called *pieds et paquets* consists of the trotters and stomach of sheep, while *rognons blanc* is sheep testicles. These are considered delicacies.

In smaller towns, butchers may double as charcutiers, offering one or two hot meat products daily, including *gaillettes* (game patties), rotisseried chickens and belly-pork roulades, *poivrons farcis* (meat-stuffed peppers), and *souris d'agneau* (lamb shanks). This is the true 'fast food' of Provence.

Around many a fruit orchard, between gnarled olive trees and along rows of unpruned grape vines, you will often see splendid tawny-, black- or red-feathered pullets (*poulardes*) strutting about, surveying the broad reaches of their terrain. A diet of wild greens, insects, corn and farmhouse scraps gives their feathers a glossy depth, and their flesh much character. Such chickens need little effort to become a splendid meal. This recipe, using lots of garlic, which mellows to sweet mildness, is balanced by the salty sharpness of anchovies and capers, and unified by wine. Serve unaccompanied, but follow it with salad, cheese, a country tart and a *trou* (literally a 'hit' or shot) of *marc de Provence*. This is a feast worthy of a dauphin.

chicken with forty garlic cloves
poularde aux quarante gousses d'ail

Wash the chicken and pat dry inside and out with kitchen paper. Rub half the olive oil over the bird and season inside and out with salt and pepper. Push the herbs inside the cavity.

Preheat the oven to 200°C (400°F) Gas 6.

Scatter the anchovies into a flameproof casserole. Put in the chicken, breast up, and put the garlic and capers all around it. Roast the bird, uncovered, for 30 minutes. Remove the heads of garlic: they should be tender inside the skins, so pop one out to check. Turn the bird breast down and baste with the juices in the pan. Reduce the heat to 180°C (350°F) Gas 4, and cook, still uncovered, for 35–40 minutes more.

To test for readiness, check that the leg joints feel loose, and that the juices run clear gold when the thigh is pierced. Alternatively, test with a meat thermometer: the temperature when inserted in the thigh should be 70°C (165°F). Once cooked, tilt the chicken and pour its internal juices into the casserole. Transfer the bird and reserved garlic to a warm place, cover and let rest for 5–8 minutes.

Pour the wine into the casserole, place over a high heat and cook for 2–3 minutes, scraping the sediment as it reduces. Squeeze 8 garlic cloves out of their skin and mash into the jus. Season if necessary.

Serve the chicken garnished with fresh thyme, and offer the jus separately. Give each diner a whole garlic head (base removed) for squeezing over their share of the carved chicken.

To drink: Pinot Noir, spicy red Primitivo from southern Italy, a substantial Shiraz rosé or a New World Chardonnay.

1.5-kg farm-reared, free-range, ideally corn-fed chicken

2 tablespoons extra virgin olive oil

a handful of fresh thyme sprigs, plus extra to garnish

6 salted anchovies, boned and chopped, or 12 canned anchovy fillets

5 heads of pink or white garlic, bases trimmed flat to expose the interior, but replaced for cooking

50 g tiny capers

125 ml robust, earthy red wine, such as Merlot or Shiraz

salt and freshly ground black pepper

Serves 4

garlic heads in their skin
ails en chemises

To poach: Trim the base and top a little if very dense. Put in a saucepan, add water or stock and simmer, covered, for 20 minutes, or until soft and fragrant.

To roast: Trim the base and top slightly if very dense. Tuck the heads upside down around and under the edges of roasting meat or poultry. Drizzle with a little olive oil. Roast at 180°C (350°F) Gas 4 for 20–30 minutes. Cover with foil if the temperature is any higher, or remove part-way through cooking.

To cook in charcoal embers: Wrap the garlic heads in a piece of wetted kitchen paper, then enclose in a double layer of foil. Seal tightly. Bury near the edge of the embers, or set on a rack a little above. Cook for 20–25 minutes, depending on the heat of the fire, or until soft. Unwrap carefully.

To microwave: Pierce every clove with a skewer. Slice off the woody base. Wrap each prepared bulb in some wetted greaseproof paper. Put into a heatproof container, evenly spaced, with 90 ml boiling water. Cook on HIGH for 12–16 minutes, or until fragrant and soft. Unwrap carefully.

Note: The garlic skin can burst if not pierced before microwave cooking. Very woody bases can overheat and burn if cooked without water.

chicken sauté Provence-style
sauté de poulet à la provençale

a1.5-kg frying chicken, cut into
10 or 12 pieces

4 tablespoons extra virgin olive oil

1 onion, sliced

100 ml medium-dry white or rosé wine

1 fresh bouquet garni: oregano, marjoram,
bay and basil, tied together

350 g ripe, flavoursome tomatoes, peeled
and chopped

2 tablespoons tomato purée

12 salt-cured black olives, lightly crushed

4 garlic cloves, finely chopped

a small handful of fresh parsley, finely
chopped, or a mixture of fresh herbs

salt and freshly ground black pepper

Serves 4–6

In the Vaucluse area of Provence, tomatoes are nicknamed *pommes d'amour* –
love apples – and this dish, which includes lots of them, certainly inspires
affection. Lots of little towns proudly proclaim their passions for certain foods:
names such as 'gourd-eaters' or 'tart-gluttons' are not unusual. This dish of
pan-cooked chicken might once have been made outdoors, over a wood fire.
If possible, try to use a youngish chicken, ideally one raised in the open, its diet
enriched by corn, for the most characterful results.

Pat dry the chicken pieces and rub all over with salt and pepper. Heat the oil in a very
large, heavy-based frying pan or a flameproof casserole. Fry half the chicken over a high
heat for 10 minutes, pressing the pieces down hard for maximum contact with the pan,
and turning them often until golden brown. Transfer the chicken to a plate, and cook the
second batch in the same way. Set aside with the first lot.

Put the onion in the pan and fry for 1 minute, stirring. Pour in the wine and add the
bouquet garni, scraping up the sediment as the wine reduces by half. Add the tomatoes,
tomato purée and olives, and cook for 3–5 minutes on a high heat, stirring. Return the
chicken to the pan, cover with foil or a lid and cook for 8–10 minutes, or until very tender.

Mix the garlic and parsley together, then scatter this topping (persillade) over the chicken
and serve hot.

To drink: A New World unoaked or lightly oaked Chardonnay, or a Sémillon.

quails with figs
cailles aux figues

Once upon a time, thrushes, larks and other little songbirds were prized as food, and considered special little treats. Quail, guinea fowl, partridge, pigeon and even baby poussin have become popular substitutes for the now-forbidden songbirds. Must – grape juice before fermentation is complete – or verjuice, the acidic juice extracted from large unripened grapes, will make the dish authentic, but are not essential. Make sure you use aromatic herbs and honey.

Pat dry the quail inside and out with kitchen paper. Season well all over, then lay the strips of bacon or ham over the breast of each bird, if not already barded. Push some fennel into the cavities, and drizzle a little honey over the top.

Heat the olive oil in a flameproof casserole and brown the birds, two at a time, over a high heat for 3–4 minutes; they should be lightly golden. When all the birds are browned, put them in the pan on their side. Pour in the grape must, let it sizzle and hiss, then add the onions and garlic. Cover the pan, reduce the heat to low and leave to cook for 15 minutes.

Turn the quails over, and tuck the figs and vine leaves all around them. Scatter with the fennel seeds, then cover and cook for 5–8 minutes more, or until the figs are hot and the birds well done. Lift out the quails, figs, vine leaves and onions and keep hot. Boil down the liquid until it's syrupy, then drizzle over the birds and serve hot with an accompaniment of your choice.

To drink: A New World Pinot Noir, a Chilean Carmenère or an Argentinian Malbec.

4 oven-ready quail, barded with bacon (if available) or 4 slices of cured raw ham for unbarded birds

1 handful of fresh fennel or dill

2 teaspoons clear, flower-scented honey

2 tablespoons extra virgin olive oil

300 ml grape must or verjuice, or red grape juice

2 small red onions, halved

2 garlic cloves, chopped

4 black or green figs, quartered lengthways

1 teaspoon fennel seeds or dill seeds, pan-toasted until aromatic

6–8 fresh vine leaves (optional)

salt and freshly ground black pepper

pearl barley, spelt or wild rice, to serve

Serves 4

Sisteron-style roast lamb
rôti d'agneau façon de Sisteron

Haute-Provence is richly supplied with superb historic towns and cities.
One such is Sisteron, known since Roman times as the 'gateway to Provence'.
Fortified for millennia, it has a strategic position, sitting at the foot of a deep
fissure in the rock created by the Durance river. Above the town towers the
dramatic Rocher de Baume. Many flocks of sheep dot the high pastures nearby,
nibbling wild thyme and other mountain herbs sometimes called *le garrigue*.
A famous local breed is the Préalpes sheep, with a long head, spindly legs and
sparse wool. The quality of its meat is exceptional: tender and tasty.

650 g large baking potatoes, peeled
a handful of fresh thyme, rosemary or marjoram
4 garlic cloves, peeled and sliced
3–4 tablespoons extra virgin olive oil
1 leg of lamb, ideally from a herb-fed, mountain breed, about 2–2.2 kg
200 ml lamb stock or water
1 x 50-g can anchovy fillets
1 small handful of fresh parsley, scissor-snipped
freshly ground sea salt and black pepper

Serves 4–6

Preheat the oven to 220°C (425°F) Gas 7.

Cut the potatoes into 5-mm slices. Arrange them in overlapping lines or circles in a
roasting tin or ovenproof dish. Put half the herb sprigs into the centre of the potato. Strip
the leaves from the rest, put in a mortar with the garlic and pound to a pulp. Add a
tablespoon of the olive oil and mix again. Rub this mixture all over the lamb, then put the
joint on top of the potatoes

Pour over the remaining oil mixed with the stock or water. Drizzle the anchovy oil all over
the potatoes, and dot the fillets about on top.

Roast, uncovered, for 30 minutes. Reduce the temperature to 160°C (325°F) Gas 3 and
continue to cook for another hour, or until the lamb is golden outside and pink at the bone.
A meat thermometer should read 65–70°C (150–160°F). Let rest for 10 minutes, then
scatter parsley over all.

Slice the lamb thickly and serve with the potatoes.

To drink: A northern Rhône red, such as Côte Rôtie, Hermitage or St-Joseph; or a great
Médoc wine, such as Pauillac or Saint-Estèphe. A Chianti Classico or Rioja Reserva would
also do the job.

Mediterranean cooking would be unthinkable without aromatic herbs: their beauty, diversity and fragrance permeate deep into the collective psyche, as well as into the cooking pot. Medicinal, curative and symbolic (thyme sprigs hung by a maiden's door were once love tokens from an admirer), herbs are one of the joys of Provence. Think of the ravishingly pretty lavender fields, the pungent basil, tarragon and rosemary scenting the air at every weekend market or the *garrigue* – wild, scrubby herb plants, stretching up into the Alpilles of Haute-Provence, and used to flavour all sorts of meat, including game. Lamb and mutton taste splendid when teamed with these *garrigue* herbs: wild thyme, oregano, bay, savory, even wild juniper. A little wild garlic leaf, if available, might also be added.

shoulder of lamb with mountain herbs
épaule d'agneau en garrigue

1.75–2-kg shoulder of lamb, ideally from a rare breed

4 garlic cloves, crushed

6 canned anchovy fillets

a small handful of fresh thyme leaves

a small handful of fresh oregano or marjoram leaves, chopped

a small handful of fresh mint leaves, chopped

100 g fresh breadcrumbs

2 tablespoons Dijon mustard, plus extra to serve

4 tablespoons salted capers, rinsed and dried

salt and freshly ground black pepper

a handful of fresh wild garlic, sorrel, chard or borage greens

6 tablespoons red wine

a little stock or water

cornichons (tiny gherkins)

6 satay sticks or wooden cocktail sticks

40 cm fine string

Serves 6–8

Get your butcher to remove all tendons and tough connective tissue from the joint. Also ask him to slip a knife around and under the blade bone to create 2 neat pockets; this will nearly sever the joint, but keep it attached at one edge.

Put the garlic, anchovies, thyme, oregano and mint into a food processor and pulse, in short bursts, until roughly chopped. Add the breadcrumbs, mustard, capers and seasoning. Pulse repeatedly until roughly mixed.

Preheat the oven to 220°C (425°F) Gas 7.

Push the garlic greens up inside the two pockets, one above and one below the bone, and add half the breadcrumb stuffing to each one. Secure the two edges of the meat by skewering with the satay sticks. Criss-cross the string around these to keep everything in place, and fasten with a knot.

Place the lamb in a large roasting tin and pour in the wine. Roast for 30 minutes, then reduce the heat to 180°C (350°F) Gas 4, and cook for 50–55 minutes more. (As a guide, allow 15 minutes per 450 g after the initial 30-minute hot-roasting.)

Remove the satay sticks and string from the cooked lamb, and let the joint stand in a warm place for 5–8 minutes.

Add a little boiling water or stock to the pan juices, if necessary, stir well, then pour into a sauce boat. Offer cornichons and Dijon mustard as accompaniments.

Note: Adding crumbs to a herb-leaf stuffing is not authentically Provençal, but in this situation it works splendidly; both pockets are plumply stuffed.

To drink: A little Côtes du Rhône-Villages or southern Rhône wine, such as Vacqueyras, Gigondas or Rasteau, or perhaps a Rioja.

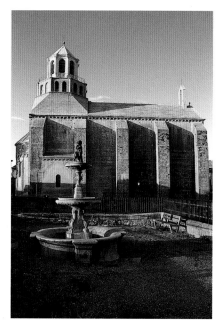

Nothing could bring your dinner guests a greater whiff of Provence than lifting the lid off this splendid *daube*: aromas of beef, wine, herbs, pork and the tantalizing fragrance of orange fill the air. The classic cooking pot used in Provence is a *daubière*, a high, round-bellied, handsomely glazed earthenware vessel, with a tight-fitting lid. It is, by custom, never washed, but wiped scrupulously clean. To keep the meat moist, a pig's trotter or sheet of pork rind may be placed on top before cooking. Sometimes a doughy paste of flour and water is used to seal the lid. In the absence of a *daubière*, use a very large, flameproof casserole. As for the meat, go to a really good butcher and get the best beef you can buy.

classic Provençal beef daube with pasta
boeuf en daube provençale et macaronnade

2 kg shin, blade or topside of beef, cut 3–4 cm thick

125-g piece of pork back fat, for larding, chilled

5 garlic cloves, quartered lengthways

a handful of fresh thyme

4 tablespoons extra virgin olive oil

750 ml robust red wine

250-g pork or bacon rind, in one piece

25 g dried ceps, morels or other dried wild mushrooms

3 carrots, halved crossways and lengthways

3 onions, quartered

100 g black olives

1 fresh bouquet garni: thyme, bay, parsley, celery and 30-cm sliver of orange zest, tied together

350 g ripe red tomatoes, peeled and chopped, or use canned plum tomatoes, chopped

4 tablespoons marc de Provence or cognac

250 g dried macaroni, to serve

Serves 8–10

Cut the beef into chunky, egg-sized pieces, each about 35–45 g. Slice the pork fat into batons: about 20 or 25.

With the point of a small, sharp knife, deeply pierce each piece of meat; as you do so, twist the blade and insert a baton of fat, a piece of garlic and a little sprig of thyme. (This is a very simplified method of larding.)

Put the beef into a deep, non-metallic bowl, add the olive oil and turn the meat until coated. Pour in 250 ml of the wine. Stir briefly, cover and let marinate at room temperature for about 4 hours.

Put the pork rind into a colander in the sink and pour some boiling water over to blanch it. Put the dried mushrooms into a saucepan with some hand-hot water. Bring to simmering point, then turn off the heat and let stand.

Once the meat has marinated, start layering the ingredients as follows in a very large, flameproof casserole: put the carrots in the bottom, then the onions, the mushrooms and their liquid and half the olives. Add half the beef with its marinade. Put the bouquet garni in the centre and cover with half the tomatoes. Make another layer of meat, and cover with the remaining tomatoes and olives.

Mix together the remaining 500 ml wine and the marc and pour over everything in the pot. Put the pork rind, skin side up, on top and close the casserole. Place on the hob and bring to a very gentle simmer: about 20–30 minutes. Preheat the oven to 160°C (325°F) Gas 3. Transfer the pot to the oven and cook, undisturbed, for 3 hours, until the beef is tender.

Just before serving, cook the pasta in a large saucepan filled with boiling salted water until al dente. Serve it alongside the daube. The juices can be ladled over as a first course.

To drink: A northern Rhône red, an Australian Shiraz or a claret.

Just south of Arles, the river Rhône splits in two: held in the 'embrace' of these twin waterways is the area known as Petite Camargue – a region of plains, dunes, rice paddies and reed-fringed swamps. Here are found pink flamingos, white herons, white horses, black bulls and *gardians* (the cowboys who tend them). Sinti and Roma (gypsy) people gather yearly in nearby Saintes-Maries-de-la-Mer, an event now world famous. This beef stew echoes that fascinating locale.

'cowboy' beef stew
boeuf gardian

Cut the meat into 2-cm pieces. Put it into a large, non-metallic bowl with the garlic, salt and pepper, turning to distribute these seasonings.

Make a slash across each onion and wedge a bay leaf lengthways in the cut. Press in 2 cloves. Tuck the onions and most of the thyme around the meat. Pour in the wine, half the cognac and all the olive oil. Stir, then cover and let marinate for 2–4 hours. Pour into a colander placed over a bowl.

Sizzle the bacon in a large flameproof casserole over a high heat until the fat runs. Remove and set aside. In the same pan, sauté the beef over a high heat in 2 batches, 6–8 minutes per batch.

Return the bacon to the pan, and add the marinade, its aromatics and the stock. Bring almost to boiling point, then reduce to a simmer, cover and cook for 2 hours. Check the liquid level after 1 hour and add 60–90 ml water if necessary.

Uncover the stew and increase the heat to medium-high. Put the potato flour into a cup, add the remaining cognac and stir well. Pour into the stew, then tilt and rotate the pan over the heat (avoid stirring if possible) until the sauce is glossy and thickened. Garnish the stew with bay leaves and serve with rice.

To drink: A muscular Spanish red, such as Ribera del Duero, an Italian Barolo, or a turbo-charged Australian Shiraz.

1 kg blade, skirt or topside of bull beef (called *taureau* beef in France), cut 2 cm thick

4 garlic cloves, crushed to a pulp

1 teaspoon sea salt flakes (fleur de sel)

½ teaspoon freshly ground black pepper

4 medium onions

4 fresh bay leaves, plus extra to garnish

8 cloves

a small bunch of fresh thyme

250 ml robust red wine

100 ml cognac

2 tablespoons extra virgin olive oil

4 slices of rindless unsmoked bacon, quartered

1 litre beef stock

2 tablespoons potato flour or arrowroot

red Camargue rice, white rice or a mixture, to serve

Serves 6–8

During November and December, outside traditional *boucheries* (butchers' shops) in the Alpes-de-Haute-Provence and down into the Var, you sometimes see bunches of wild herbs and ribbons attached to the carcass of a magnificently handsome, bristly brown-, black- and white-haired creature with a mighty head and black hoofs. This is a *sanglier*, or wild boar. Often it stays on display for several days, until all the orders for it have been taken. It is then butchered with due ceremony and carried off to be cooked with respect. Wild boar usually needs a substantial amount of barding or larding with bacon or pork fat to prevent dryness, since long cooking is essential. The result is a rich, dark and gamey stew. Dried fruit and walnuts add distinction to this version.

wild boar stew
estouffade de sanglier

1.5 kg wild boar meat, shoulder or haunch

1 teaspoon coarse salt

20 black peppercorns

12 juniper berries

2 dried bay leaves, crumbled

250 g bacon lardons, cut into small cubes

250 g baby onions or shallots, blanched and peeled

75 g dried apricots, opened out flat

75 g walnut halves

75 g small black olives

500 ml medium-dry red wine

250 ml pork, veal or chicken stock

1 fresh bouquet garni: thyme, parsley, celery and oregano, tied together

2 tablespoons génépy, anisette or absinthe (optional)

vegetable purée, spelt, risotto or pasta, to serve

Serves 6–8

Cut the meat into cubes 2–3 cm square, discarding any tough cartilage and connective tissue.

Using a pestle and mortar, pound the salt, pepper, juniper berries and bay leaves to a powder. Toss the meat in this mixture and let stand.

Heat the lardons in a large, flameproof casserole over a high heat until their fat runs. Use a slotted spoon to transfer the bacon to a plate.

Sauté the wild boar meat in the bacon fat in 2 batches, 4–5 minutes for each batch. Transfer the meat to a plate and set aside.

Put the onions into the pan and sauté for 2–3 minutes. Add half the apricots, half the walnuts and half the olives, then return half the lardons to the pan.

Spoon in half the wild boar meat. Put the remaining apricots, walnuts, olives and lardons on top. Add the remaining meat, then pour in the wine and stock, and push the bouquet garni well down in it. Bring the pan to a gentle simmer, then cover, reduce the heat to very low and cook for 1½–2 hours.

Uncover the casserole and check the liquid level: the meat should be nearly covered. Test the meat for tenderness: if slightly chewy, allow 30–45 minutes more. The liquid should become sticky and rich, and the meat very tender.

At serving time, drizzle in the alcohol (if using), but do not stir. Bring the pan to a lively simmer, then tilt to mix the flavours evenly.

Serve the stew hot with a purée of celeriac, parsnip or pumpkin. Some spelt, risotto or ribbon pasta would also be suitable.

Note: Any juices remaining from this stew can be served the following day, poured over wide ribbon noodles, gnocchi or rice.

To drink: A Cabernet Sauvignon or a restrained Merlot would work well here.

rabbit cooked with savory
lapin à la pebre d'ail

Pebre d'ail is one of the Provençal names for winter savory or *sariette*. Another is *poivre d'âne* (*pebre d'ase* in Niçois dialect), meaning 'donkey's pepper'. It needs pounding to make it suitable for eating, as it is naturally tough and prickly, but it is a favourite herb for use with rabbit, which is frequently cooked as a *gibelotte* (stew). Mustard is also popular with rabbit, and this, together with egg yolks and cream, gives a velvety *blanquette* effect in the recipe below.

Pat dry the rabbit with kitchen paper. Halve the leg joints, if large, to give 7 or 9 portions.

Using a pestle and mortar, pound together the salt, savory, peppercorns and cayenne (if using) until you have a powder. Rub this mixture all over the rabbit.

Put the rabbit, wine and stock into a medium flameproof casserole and bring to the boil. Reduce the heat to a simmer, then cover and cook for 20 minutes.

Add the potatoes, pushing them down into the liquid. Cover the pan and cook for 20 minutes more, or until the rabbit is tender and the potatoes cooked. Lift out and drain the rabbit and potatoes. Keep hot.

In a heatproof bowl, whisk together the mustard, egg yolks and crème fraîche. Pour in a ladleful of the hot stock mixture, whisk well, then return this liquid to the pan. Cook over a low to medium heat for 3–4 minutes, or until the sauce is creamy and thick. Do not let it boil.

Return the rabbit to the pan. Reheat for 1 minute, then serve hot with the vegetables of your choice.

Note: No savory? Substitute thyme and a bit of marjoram with a pinch of cayenne. Alternatively, use a bunch of fresh tarragon at the simmering stage.

To drink: A broader-tasting, older Riesling or a Pinot Noir.

1 tender rabbit, about 800 g–1.25 kg prepared weight, jointed

½ teaspoon coarse sea salt

6 sprigs of fresh winter savory, scissor-snipped

8 white peppercorns, plus a pinch of cayenne pepper (optional)

450 ml medium-dry white wine

250 ml chicken or veal stock

350 g small, new-season's potatoes, peeled

4 tablespoons Dijon mustard

2 large egg yolks

100 g crème fraîche

boiled baby carrots or turnips, or green beans, to serve

Serves 4

High in the rugged, forested areas of the Var, deer are sometimes glimpsed through the undergrowth. *La chasse* is the traditional autumn and winter preoccupation, as is wild mushroom foraging and chestnut gathering, and wild venison is a popular dish. For city dwellers further south, however, it is now easy to buy small cuts of neatly trimmed venison, wild or farmed, from butchers, charcuteries and even supermarkets. Being lean, tender venison needs minimal cooking as it can dry out easily. This recipe, which requires it to be flash-fried and served with a wine glaze, probably takes it name from the colour of a camel's coat, as both are tawny brown.

venison steaks with cameline sauce
médaillons de chevreuil à la sauce cameline

4 medallions of venison, each about 120 g

2 garlic cloves, chopped

1 teaspoon black peppercorns

½ teaspoon ground mixed spice

½ teaspoon freshly grated nutmeg

4 canned anchovy fillets, chopped

4 sprigs of fresh rosemary

2 teaspoons wildflower or lavender honey

2 teaspoons red wine vinegar

100 g pain d'épice (spice cake) or gingerbread, or ginger biscuits, crumbled

1 tablespoon cognac

2 teaspoons concentrated beef bouillon or rich stock

50 g butter or lard

90 ml robust red wine

50 g redcurrant, crab apple, guava or quince jelly

leafy salad, to serve (optional)

Serves 4

Pat dry the medallions with kitchen paper. Slice each horizontally into 3 pieces. Set aside.

Put the garlic, peppercorns, spice, nutmeg and anchovies into a mortar and pound to a paste with a pestle. Scissor-snip the leaves from a rosemary sprig directly into this mixture. Pound again, then stir in the honey and vinegar. Rub this mixture over both sides of the meat slices. Let stand for 5 minutes.

Put the cake or biscuits into a food processor and whizz for 30 seconds. Tip the crumbs into a bowl and stir in the cognac, a teaspoonful at a time. Do the same with the bouillon. It should be a damp, crumbly mass. Set aside.

Heat the butter in a heavy-based frying pan until sizzling. Cook the dry-marinated venison for no more than 50–60 seconds on each side, pushing the meat down firmly as it cooks. Transfer to a plate and keep hot.

Pour the wine into the pan, followed by the redcurrant jelly and 4 tablespoons of boiling water. Stir and scrape up the sediment. Cook over a low heat until the mixture becomes sticky. Briefly turn the hot venison in this glaze.

Serve the venison in a pool of the glaze with a mound of spicy crumbs alongside. Garnish with sprigs of rosemary. A garlicky mixed leaf salad dressed with walnut oil would be an excellent accompaniment.

To drink: A Châteauneuf-du-Pape; a rich sweet Cabernet-Carmenère blend or an Australian Cabernet-Shiraz blend.

Veal, though considered a delicacy in France, is rated as less important than beef and lamb in Provence, unless it is stuffed with a highly aromatic, herb-scented stuffing. Lemon, integral to the Côte d'Azur, and particularly associated with Menton, where each year a lemon festival is held, makes a perfect seasoning for the wild and fresh herbs in these individual veal parcels. Served hot, they suit green vegetables. Eaten cold, they should be sliced and served with salad; they look like small, earthy terrines.

veal parcels in lemon sauce
paupiettes de veau au citron

4 veal escalopes, about 900 g total weight

300 g lean veal, cubed

300 g minced pork

6 tablespoons crème fraîche

juice and grated zest of 1 lemon

1 handful of fresh herbs, including chervil parsley, tarragon and chives, if possible

2 garlic cloves, chopped

1 teaspoon black peppercorns

1 teaspoon sea salt crystals

75 g unsalted butter

2 teaspoons anchovy paste (page 16)

1 tablespoon extra virgin olive oil

4 tablespoons concentrated chicken or pork bouillon

baby asparagus, green beans or broccoli, to serve

16 wooden cocktail sticks
fine string, for shaping

Serves 4

Put the escalopes, one at a time, between two sheets of clingfilm and roll gently into a circular shape with a rolling pin until very thin indeed. Carefully peel off the clingfilm and cut each escalope in half.

Put the cubed veal, minced pork, crème fraîche, half the lemon zest and half the herbs, scissor-snipped, into a food processor. Pulse briefly to create an evenly mixed stuffing. Do not overprocess.

Put the garlic, peppercorns and salt into a mortar and pound to a fine grit. Sprinkle half of this into the stuffng and process again briefly.

Mix the other half of the garlic mixture with most of the remaining herbs (scissor-snipped), the butter and anchovy paste. Shape into a log, wrap in foil and fast-freeze it until set. Transfer to the fridge until needed.

Spoon a mound of stuffing mixture onto each of the 8 escalope pieces. Wrap the meat around the stuffing to form a ball, and secure using 2 cocktail sticks.

Turn the parcels right side up. Criss-cross the string around them twice more, keeping the shape plump, and knot carefully. Discard the cocktail sticks.

Heat the oil over a medium heat in a heavy-based frying pan, then brown the parcels for 3 minutes on each side. Pour in the lemon juice and bouillon, add 150 ml water and bring to a lively simmer. Reduce to a gentle simmer, then cover with a lid or foil and cook for 18–20 minutes. Check that they are cooked through.

Slice the savoury butter into 8 discs and put 1 on each parcel just before serving. Scatter with the remaining zest shreds and garnish with the remaining herbs. Serve delicate green vegetables on the side.

To drink: Châteauneuf-du-Pape red or white; a good Chablis or other white Burgundy or a cool-climate Chardonnay from Russian River, California or from Casablanca Valley, Chile.

desserts et fromage

sweet things and cheese

sweet confections and their rituals

Many of the outrageously sweet and delicious foodstuffs that are most strongly associated with Provence are used in various celebratory rituals. The most well known of these is the feast held on Christmas Eve: *Le Grand Souper* (*Lou Gros Soupa* in dialect) at which the extended family gathers. This is a *maigre* (meatless or lean) meal, as dictated by religion, and very elaborate. Many of Provence's best fruits (fresh and dried), nuts, confections and sweet things are represented in the numerous desserts served at its second part. So are its sweet wines.

The ritual
Following a visit to church for midnight mass, the table is set with three tablecloths representing the Trinity of Father, Son and Holy Ghost. Three candlesticks are lit. Holly branches with red berries (but never any mistletoe – it's bad luck), beautiful wood roses and some green shoots of St Barbara's wheat, sown before the saint's feast day on 4 December, are set on the table.

The first candle is extinguished. One tablecloth comes off. Now come the seven courses representing the seven sufferings of Mary. The supper is served with 13 bread rolls, representing Jesus and the 12 Apostles, and the seven lean courses are followed by the famous 13 desserts.

The seven courses
1. First comes a soup called Aigo Boulido (page 64), rich with garlic.
2. Next come snails in a broth flavoured with tomatoes. (In Arles, they are served with aïoli instead.)
3. Salt cod or eel comes next, often served in Raïto sauce, rich with red wine, tomatoes, anchovies and olives (see page 80). Mullet sometimes follows this.

4. A simple omelette.

5. Now come classic vegetables, raw or cooked: cauliflower, chard stalks, cardoons, celery and artichokes with Aïoli (see page 15) or Anchoïade (see page 16).

6. Curly endive salad containing garlicky croutons.

7. This final course consists of not one, but 13, desserts.

At this stage, the second tablecloth is removed and the second candle flame is blown out.

The 13 Desserts (*Les Treize Desserts*)

1. *Fougasse*, a slashed flat bread, also called *pompe à l'huile,* or ladder bread or *gibassier*. This is made from flour, sugar, yeast, olive oil, orange flower water and citrus zest.

2. White nougat with hazelnuts, pine nuts and pistachios: Provence is famous for this.

3. Black nougat: a sort of praline made from caramelized honey and nuts (see page 134).

Next come the dried fruit and nuts, called the *quatre mendiants* (four beggars), which actually refer to the four great Roman Catholic religious orders and their colours.

4. Dried figs representing Franciscans.

5. Raisins representing Dominicans.

6. Almonds representing Carmelites.

7. Hazelnuts representing Augustinians.

Next come the six fruits.

8. First are grapes, often stored in the attic until semi-dried.

9. Quinces or quince paste, or perhaps apples.

10. Fresh oranges, clementines or mandarins.

11. Calissons (see page 122) or candied citrons or mandarins.

12. Pears or pomegranates (or dates or prunes), symbols of the Orient.

13. Oreillettes: light, crisp pastries (see page 141).

Carthagène, a fortified, spiced red wine drink, along with fruit liqueurs, particularly cherry ratafia (see page 148), are offered throughout the meal.

At last, the four corners of the third tablecloth are gathered up and wrap any leftovers of the supper. These will go to 'the poor'.

Versions of this intricate ceremony still take place all over Provence each Christmas.

Almonds and honey

Who would have thought a nut could be so versatile? Not only are almonds eaten green as a vegetable in the spring, but ripe and dried, they feature in many savoury sauces and spreads, are added to a wide variety of sweet biscuits, cakes and pastries, and are the basis of marzipan.

Flowering almond trees, along with cultivated lavender, which so often thrives nearby in gorgeous purple rows, help to give Provençal honey its intense, distinctive floral notes. It is important for the bees to be near the flowers at the right time, as the nectar is secreted on only ten days of the year. Producers must therefore move their hives – up to 400 of them – around the countryside. For this reason, they often call themselves 'honey shepherds', taking their 'flocks' of bees to the best 'grazing'.

Mono-floral (single-flower) honey, from the nectar of acacia, chestnut, lavender, thyme and broom blossoms, is prized, particularly if it is *miel de cru* – from one single area. Poly-floral (mixed-flower) honey is made throughout the year and is less distinctive. Use delicious Provençal honeys as a spread on toast or bread, drizzled over cheese, as a sweetener for tea and tisanes (see page 149), in sauces or as a glaze for game.

Calissons d'Aix

These pretty, almond-shaped biscuit confections, produced in and around Puyricard near Aix, are some of the most distinctive in France. Under pearly white icing is bitter-sweet almond paste flavoured with crystallized melon, orange and apricot, depending on season. Underneath is white rice paper. Each is about 10–14 g: a perfect bite.

Chocolate

Valrhona chocolate, a famous brand produced in Provence, was created in 1924 by a chef from the Rhône valley, hence the name Valrhona (previously it was called La Chocolaterie de Vivarais). It produces excellent chocolate with a high proportion of cocoa solids, essential for making certain cakes and desserts. Like wine producers, the company even offers a 'single cru' product, which is made from cocoa beans gathered in one place. One such is Guanaja, which contains 70 per cent cocoa solids. Vintage

chocolates, from unique sources, are recent creations. Another good Provençal producer is Chocolatier Manon, near Forcalquier.

Crystallized fruits

The towns of Apt, Carpentras, Cotignac and Beaumes-de-Venise are among a select group of places famous for producing superb crystallized fruits. The process of infusing fresh fruits with sugar is an amazingly elaborate and drawn-out process, and you can witness it yourself on the guided tours offered by some producers. The fruits look like glistening jewellery, and the best examples are true to the colour, taste, texture and aroma of the originals. Crystallized clementines, mandarins, orange segments, pears, figs, apricots, cherries, plums, chestnuts, pineapple rings and slices of *cédrat* are eaten as a dessert, added to ice creams and cakes, and even used to stuff ravioli.

Floral confections, syrups and conserves

Flowers and herb stems or leaves can be sugar-dipped, then candied to crisp. I have enjoyed violets and rose petals, and the blossoms of acacia, jasmine and angelica treated in this way. Flower syrups, made from poppies, violets and roses, add elegance to cocktails and desserts. Conserves and jams scented with bergamot, rose petal and jasmine are delicious on toast, or in game sauces or gravies.

Nougat

Montélimar has been the centre of nougat production in Provence since the 16th century. White nougat, which is a mixture of honey, glucose and sugar syrup cooked to a very specific stage, then blended with egg whites, icing sugar and water, can be very soft or chewy. Nuts and dried fruits may also be added. The Provençal habit is to slice and layer it into desserts, add it to ice creams, nibble it with a coffee, tea, tisane or a glass of sweet wine or eat it on its own. Black Nougat (see page 134) is more like praline. Unlike white nougat, it sets hard and is broken into bits to be used for decorating desserts.

Other regional sweetstuffs

Fascinating honey cakes, *pains d'épice* (spice cakes), *croquants* (crunchy biscuits), hard, sweet biscuits, such as *navettes* (bobbin-shaped) are frequently seen in markets. Multi-coloured marzipan layered cakes and sweetmeats of meringue and of nougat or hard caramel are popular. There are famous candies local to particular areas or Provence, such as *berlingots* (from Carpentras) made in many different flavours and colours.

Truly outstanding ice creams and sorbets are produced seasonally in Provence. Summer–autumn flavours may include such delights as white peach, cassis, apricot, lavender, rose, lemon, verbena and pistachio.

FRAMBOISE
3.50€ pièce
6€ les 2

FRAISE
3.50€ pièce
6€ les 2

miel de romarin

Muriel et Roland DOUAY
Apiculteurs
84240 GRAMBOIS
☎ 04 90 07 37 14

miel d'or

Muriel et Roland DOUAY
Apiculteurs
84240 GRAMBOIS
☎ 04 90 07 37 14

peaches in rose syrup
pêches au sirop de vin rosé

Voluptuous, blushy-pink peaches in a syrup of flower-scented rosé wine are a wonderfully indulgent dessert. *Calissons d'Aix* – eye-shaped candied sweetmeats sold in lozenge-shaped boxes – are made all over Provence. First recorded at the 1473 wedding feast of King René, they were apparently an attempt to gladden the heart of the bride-to-be. Almonds, candied melon and boiled honey syrup go into the mix, as do candied orange, mandarin and apricot. Rice paper bases and snowy white icing complete the picture. These, with the poached peaches and rose petal decoration, create a blissful dessert.

4 large, ripe peaches, ideally white-fleshed
400 ml medium-sweet rosé wine, ideally Provençal
75 g clear wildflower honey, preferably garrigue-scented
1 teaspoon rosewater
75 ml marc de Provence
16 sugared rose petals or fresh pink rose petals, to serve (optional)
8 Calissons d'Aix biscuits, to serve

Serves 4

Rub the fuzzy layer from the peach skin. Make a criss-cross cut at the stalk end and the base of each peach.

Put the wine, honey and rosewater in a deep, medium-sized saucepan big enough to hold the peaches in a single layer. Bring this liquid to the boil.

Add the peaches and reduce the heat to a lively simmer. Splash the syrup all over the peaches as they cook, and tilt the pan to rotate them and ensure even cooking. Try to avoid stirring. Cook for 6–8 minutes minimum.

With a slotted spoon, transfer the peaches, one by one, to a plate. Pull off and discard the skin, then let the fruit cool completely.

Let the wine syrup cool, then stir in the marc.

To serve, put each peach into a bowl. Drizzle over the syrup and scatter the petals on top (if using). Offer the Calissons separately.

To drink: Sweet rosé or a Gewürztraminer (for their rosewater flavours).

sabayon with Muscat
sabayon au Muscat de Beaumes-de-Venise

In the foothills of the Dentelles de Montmirail is the village of Beaumes-de-Venise. In centuries past its fabulous golden Muscat wines are said to have tempted the eminences at the papal court of Avignon into worldly distractions; and they continue to woo us to this day. Highly alcoholic (15–20 per cent) and with an apricot-perfumed intensity, the Beaumes Muscat invites joyfulness and fun. It can be drunk iced as an aperitif (perfect with chilled *foie gras*), is superb with salty blue cheese, but is also stunning when used as the basis of a frothy dessert, such as this.

4 eggs
85 g caster sugar
grated zest of ¼ orange
60 ml Muscat de Beaumes-de-Venise
40 ml marc de Provence

To serve
4 bunches of small green grapes
8 fresh cherries
4 sprigs of whitecurrants or redcurrants
1 large slice of Cavaillon melon, sliced
2 ripe apricots or nectarines

Serves 4

Put the eggs, sugar and zest into a large, heatproof bowl and whisk the mixture until it becomes pale, frothy and high.

Quarter-fill a saucepan with boiling water and put it over a low heat. Sit the bowl of whisked eggs on top, but do not allow it to touch the water.

Mix together the Muscat and marc. Trickle this into the bowl, whisking continuously, until the mixture is warm, dense, mousse-like and much more voluminous: about 5 minutes.

Remove the bowl and let stand in some iced water to prevent overheating. Continue to whisk for 1 minute.

Spoon the sabayon into four serving glasses. Set a bunch of tiny grapes, 2 cherries, a currant sprig, a melon slice and some apricot segments around each sabayon. Serve warm.

To drink: A glass of chilled Muscat de Beaumes-de-Venise.

Apricot trees, spreading along the gently sloping banks of the Durance river, look gnarled and barren until late spring. Suddenly, velvety buds burst through and luminous blossoms appear soon after. It is a glorious sight, and one that makes you long for the ripe, sun-warmed fruit. Once summer is well advanced, it can be seen tumbling out of baskets under canvas awnings at local markets. An apricot tart, glazed and warm from the oven, is as welcome as the sun bursting through the clouds. This version, needing no flan tins or split-second timing, is an effortless dessert after a carefree day spent outdoors.

apricot tart
tarte d'abricots

375-g packet ready-rolled puff pastry, chilled

1 egg, beaten, for glazing

500 g ripe apricots, halved and stoned, the stones reserved

100 g apricot jam

1 tablespoon freshly squeezed lemon juice

4 tablespoons vanilla sugar

sifted icing sugar, to decorate (optional)

Serves 4–6

Unroll the pastry and cut out a circle 25 cm in diameter. Re-roll the offcuts and make 4 strips about 2 x 25 cm. Set aside.

Transfer the pastry to a lightly oiled baking sheet. Leaving a 2-cm border all round, prick the rest of the pastry with a fork. Preheat the oven to 220°C (425°F) Gas 7.

Brush the unpricked border of the pastry with the beaten egg. Place the pastry strips on it, cutting the ends to be joined on the diagonal and pressing them neatly together. These will puff up when baked, and act like a wall around the fruit. Brush beaten egg all over the pastry, including the pricked area. Blind bake for 20 minutes, or until golden and risen at the edges. Prick once again.

Meanwhile, crack open 6 of the apricot stones. Remove and shred the kernels.

Cut each apricot half into 6 segments. Arrange them, flesh upwards, on the pastry. Scatter the shredded kernels over the top.

Put the jam and lemon juice in a small bowl and stir until smooth. Using a pastry brush, paint this glaze all over the fruit. Sprinkle on the vanilla sugar, then bake for 20 minutes, until the apricots are soft, fragrant and slightly browned at the tips. Serve warm, dusted with icing sugar, if liked.

Note: Red plums, nectarines or peaches can be used in place of apricots, but do not use the kernels of plums.

To drink: Chilled Sauternes would be perfect.

praline-dressed roasted figs with ricotta
figues pralinés aux anis et avec brousse

Praline is an ancient confection of caramelized sugar to which chopped nuts, usually almonds, are added. Figs are a perfect partner for praline. These trees grow profusely in Provence – in walled gardens, beside ancient walls, in town squares and often at the verges of winding roads. There are many ways to enjoy figs: with cured raw ham, in jams, with blue cheeses or in this elegant dessert.

Preheat the grill to very hot. Put the figs, cut side up, on a baking sheet and sprinkle them with 25 g of the sugar, the cardamom seeds and the anise seeds. Grill for 8–10 minutes, or until hot and sizzling. Set aside.

Put the nuts on a lightly oiled baking sheet.

Heat the remaining 100 g sugar in a heavy-based frying pan over a high heat without stirring. Keep tilting the pan as the sugar melts; gradually the base layer becomes clear, then this darkens to deep gold and melts the sugar above.

Carefully drizzle streaks of this molten sugar over the nuts. (Take care – it's very hot.) Let cool and set. Crush half into praline and keep the rest for decoration.

Serve the figs with the liqueur drizzled on the plate and a scoop of ricotta alongside. Decorate with a flowering herb sprig, and scatter praline over the figs.

To drink: Herbal liqueurs like Sénacole or Verveine produced by monasteries near Cannes.

8 medium black or green figs, stem ends intact

125 g white or golden caster sugar

10 green cardamom pods, crushed and seeds extracted

1 teaspoon anise seeds, lightly crushed

50 g freshly shelled almonds or pine nuts

4 tablespoons herbal liqueur, such as Sénacole or Verveine (from L'Îsle de Lérins), or Farigoule (from Forcalquier) or pastis

250 g ricotta cheese, to serve

sprigs of fresh flowering thyme, lemon verbena, rosemary or lavender, to decorate

Serves 4–5

Menton, in the easternmost stretch of the French Riviera, has four different harvest times for the many lemon varieties that flourish there: *primofiore* (October to December), *limoni* (December to May), *verdeli* (during the summer months) and *mayolino* or *biancheto* (for autumn's cooler, dry harvest). *Quatre saisons*, a famous scented lemon, thrives all year round. No wonder, then, that Menton holds a yearly celebration, the *Fête du Citron*, at which serious awards are made and much festivity and flag-waving takes place. There is even a museum in nearby Monaco, where citrus enthusiasts gather and research. Over 400 citrus varieties are said to grow in this sunny area, including lumpy citrons, kumquats, limequats, pomelos, vivid little limes and many types of orange. The tartlets below are perfect for afternoon tea, with a coffee or tisane, or as a dessert or a celebration: in fact, any sweet occasion.

tiny lemon tarts
tartelettes au citron

75 g sifted icing sugar, plus 4 tablespoons for the topping

175 g unsalted butter, cubed, at room temperature

½ teaspoon salt

2 large free-range egg yolks

250 g sifted plain white flour

Filling and topping

4 large, free-range eggs

150 g vanilla sugar

2 tablespoons finely grated lemon zest

150 g crème fraîche, plus extra to serve

100 ml freshly squeezed lemon juice, plus 4 tablespoons extra

2 tablespoons mandarin or other citrus liqueur

6 loose-bottomed tartlet tins, 9-cm diameter

Serves 6

To make the pastry, put the icing sugar, butter, salt and egg yolks into the bowl of a food processor. Whizz for 20 seconds.

Add half the flour and pulse to mix; add the remaining flour and pulse again until the texture resembles breadcrumbs. With the machine running, trickle in 2 tablespoons iced water; the dough quickly clumps into a ball. Wrap it in clingfilm and chill for 20 minutes.

Divide the pastry into 6 equal balls. Dust with flour, then roll them out on a sheet of silicone (non-stick) paper to a thickness of 5 mm. Cut each into a circle 10–11 cm in diameter.

Preheat the oven to 180°C (350°F) Gas 4.

Place the tartlet tins on a baking sheet. Gently ease the pastry into the tins, letting it sit 1 cm above the edge: it will shrink slightly as it cooks. Line each pastry case with greaseproof paper and baking beans or rice. Bake for 15 minutes. Remove the paper and beans, then bake the cases for 5 minutes more.

Now make the filling. Put the eggs, vanilla sugar, half the zest, the crème fraîche, lemon juice and liqueur into a food processor. Pulse in brief bursts until the mixture looks even. Divide it between the 6 pastry cases.

Reduce the oven temperature to 120°C (250°F) Gas ½. Bake the tartlets for 15–20 minutes, or until the filling is barely set.

Meanwhile, prepare the topping: put the remaining zest, the 4 tablespoons of icing sugar and the extra lemon juice into a frying pan. Cook over a medium heat until the syrup reduces and smells fragrant.

Remove the tartlets from the oven and drizzle this syrup over them. Serve hot, warm or cool, adding a dusting of icing sugar, if liked, and some extra crème fraîche.

To drink: A citrus liqueur or Botrytis or late-harvest Riesling from the New World.

'Lavender is the soul of Haute-Provence,' wrote Jean Giono, the celebrated writer from Forcalquier. The intensely blue-mauve flowers and heady perfume of true lavender (*Lavandula augustifolia*) contribute greatly to the landscape's distinctive character. Even shutters are painted the same colour. Wild beds of lavender have grown for centuries on the slopes of Mount Ventoux, but these days, cultivated varieties, mainly *Lavandula latifolia*, a hybrid, are the mainstay of local production. The crop is at its most intoxicating in mid-July, when the buds burst open and the scent is released. Harvest then happens quickly and the distillation process begins. The finished product ends up in oils, perfumes, cosmetics and soaps. But lavender can also add finesse to cakes, ice creams, sweets and desserts. Be careful to use genuine (not spike) lavender, and beware of sprayed products.

lavender creams and scented syrup
crèmes de lavande parfumés avec sirop

12–15 g (about 50 stems) fresh or dried lavender (*Lavandula augustifolia*)

50 g vanilla sugar

60 ml elderflower cordial

a few drops of red and blue food colouring (optional)

60 ml dessert wine, such as Sauternes or Muscatel

1 x 7-g sachet gelatine

250 g mascarpone or cream cheese

100 ml single cream

4 small ramekins or moulds, greased with ¼ teaspoon almond oil

Serves 4

Remove the buds from 40 lavender stems and reserve the 10 remaining stems for decoration.

Put the buds and vanilla sugar into a clean electric coffee or spice grinder and whizz to create a pale mauve powder.

Put the powder into a small saucepan with 6 tablespoons (90 ml) water and the elderflower cordial. Stir over a medium heat until a thick syrup forms. Add a few drops of colouring if you want a deeper mauve, then let cool slightly. Strain to remove most of the actual blooms, and reserve the tinted syrup.

Pour the wine into a heatproof jug, sprinkle in the gelatine and leave for 10 minutes. Heat over boiling water, or in a microwave on HIGH in 20-second bursts, until the gelatine is completely dissolved.

Put the mascarpone and cream into a bowl and whisk together. Whisk in the melted gelatine and half the reserved syrup. Spoon into the prepared ramekins and smooth the tops. Chill for a minimum of 2 hours, until firmly set, or overnight.

Just before serving, wring out a cloth in very hot water, hold it around a ramekin and invert onto a clean serving plate. Add a drizzle of syrup to each dessert and 2 or 3 whole stems of lavender.

Note: If not turning out the lavender creams, they can be served in cups or glasses instead of ramekins.

To drink: A rich Sauternes or Muscat, such as Beaumes-de-Venise.

bitter chocolate ice cream with crystallized chestnuts

glace au chocolat amer avec marrons glacés

'Sweet-toothed' is how the people of Montélimar, Gargas, Sault, Apt and Aix-en-Provence describe themselves, and they're not wrong. *Nougat blanc, nougat noir, calisson* sweetmeats and artisanal chocolates are produced with pride. Superb chocolate distinguishes this ice cream.

4 marrons glacés
175 g vanilla sugar
1 teaspoon ground cinnamon
150 ml milk
350 g bitter dark chocolate, such as Valrhona (70% cocoa solids, minimum), broken up
1 tablespoon glucose syrup
1 tablespoon chocolate or nut liqueur
450 ml double cream, chilled
icing sugar and/or cocoa powder, for dusting (optional)

Serves 4

Break the marrons glacés into pieces. Put into an electric coffee or spice grinder and add 2 tablespoons of the sugar and the cinnamon. Whizz in brief bursts until the mixture becomes a powder. Set aside.

Put the milk, 250g of the chocolate and the remaining sugar into a heavy-based saucepan. Stir constantly over a low heat until the chocolate melts. Add the glucose syrup and the ground-up mixture, and stir until dissolved. Remove the pan and stand it in iced water to cool, then stir in the liqueur and cream.

Pour the mixture into a chilled ice-cream maker and churn for 20–30 minutes, or until set and creamy. Alternatively, freeze in a covered plastic container for 3 hours. Beat hard, then cover again and refreeze for another 3 hours.

Melt the remaining 100 g chocolate in a bowl over near-boiling water, or microwave on HIGH in 30-second bursts until melted. Brush a layer of the chocolate over some teflon fabric or silicone (non-stick) paper. Fast-freeze for 5 minutes, then chill until firm. Cut into various shapes, such as circles or triangles, and use to decorate the scoops of ice cream. Dust with icing sugar or cocoa, or both, if liked.

To drink: Sweet Champagne (to skitter across the tastebuds), or some chocolate or fruit liqueur.

white nougat ice cream

nougat glacé

To make white nougat at home requires patience and precision, so buy some from a reputable supplier. Black nougat (more like praline or brittle) is easier. This recipe contains both types. The result is utterly seductive.

650 ml creamy milk
7 large, free-range egg yolks
300 g clear thyme, rosemary, lavender or eucalyptus honey
⅛ teaspoon salt
300 ml double cream, lightly whipped
100 g white nougat, cut into fine slivers, plus extra to decorate
thyme, rosemary or lavender flowers, to decorate

Black nougat
100 g caster sugar
50-g mixture unblanched almonds and flaked almonds, chopped

a 700-ml rectangular loaf tin

Serves 4–6

Boil the milk. Put the egg yolks, honey and salt in a large bowl set over warm water and whisk together until pale and fluffy.

Pour in the boiling milk, stir, then return to the pan. Cook over a medium heat, whisking constantly, for about 5 minutes. Set the pan in a bowl of iced water and stir until cold. When cold, stir in the whipped cream and white nougat.

Pour the custard into a chilled ice-cream maker and churn for 35 minutes, or until nearly set. Pour into the loaf tin and freeze for 2–3 hours. Alternatively, pour into a 1.25-litre plastic container, then cover and fast-freeze for 5–6 hours.

To make the black nougat, put the sugar and 3 tablespoons water into a heavy-based frying pan and heat, without stirring, until the sugar dissolves to gold: 160°C (320°F) on a sugar thermometer. Add the almonds, stirring quickly to mix. Heat for 40–60 seconds longer: the mixture will darken, but must not burn. Pour onto a baking sheet. Let cool and set, then break into chunks to serve with the ice cream.

About 20 minutes before serving, transfer the ice cream to the fridge. When ready to serve, run a knife around the edges, then invert onto a serving plate. Serve sliced, decorated with some nougat pieces and edible, scented flowers.

To drink: Pedro Ximénez, or late-picked Eiswein from Alsace.

scented fruit jelly
gelée parfumée aux petits fruits

Tall goblets of sweet, refreshingly cool, scented wine jelly, studded with pretty little summer fruits...what could be more perfect? Aim to make this dessert when wild strawberries or *fraises de garrigue* are available: their extraordinary intensity helps to make this recipe a remarkable one.

120 ml medium-dry or sweet Champagne, or sparkling white wine

6 gelatine leaves or 1½ sachets (11 g) gelatine granules

760 ml yellow Chartreuse liqueur

100 ml Muscat de Beaumes-de-Venise

50 g wild or small cultivated strawberries, quartered

100 g raspberries

75 g redcurrants, half left on the sprigs to decorate, or 8 fresh cherries, plus 8 to decorate

4 x 150-ml champagne flutes

Serves 4

Put 100 ml of the Champagne in a heatproof measuring jug, add the gelatine and leave to soften and swell for 10 minutes. Mix the remaining Champagne with the Chartreuse and Muscat.

Heat the gelatine mixture over boiling water, or in a microwave on high in 20-second bursts, until the gelatine is completely dissolved. Pour in the Chartreuse mixture, stir, then cool over iced water. During the following steps, set the gelatine over the pan of boiling water now and again to keep it barely liquid.

Put a quarter of the strawberries into each champagne flute. Pour in a quarter of the gelatine mixture, then refrigerate until firm.

Repeat this layering process with each type of fruit, letting each layer set before adding the next. Place any remaining gelatine mixture over the iced water to set firmly, then chop it into tiny pieces.

Pile some of the chopped gelatine onto each dessert and decorate with the reserved sprigs of redcurrants or the cherries. Serve cool or chilled.

To drink: Muscat de Beaumes-de-Venise or a sweet red Mavrodaphne from Greece.

During a visit to Provence during the autumn of 2005, my husband and I went to Arles, where we stayed in one of the grandest, most splendidly eccentric hotels ever: Le Nord-Pinus. Our room, filled with flowers, fruits and photographs of famous toreadors, had a balcony that gave us a wonderful view of the town, with its museums, galleries, churches, shops, cafés and restaurants – all of which we explored at length. In several pâtisseries we found magnificent terrines of marzipan studded with nuts and seeds, and jewelled with crystallized fruits. Here is my version.

marzipan loaf in the Arles style
terrine de massepin Arlésienne

100 g shelled pistachios

200 g dried apricots

750 g natural (uncoloured) marzipan

2 tablespoons coarse sugar crystals

zest of 1 orange or 2 clementines, scissor-snipped

½ teaspoon rosewater, orange flower water or dark rum

100 g shelled pine nuts or blanched almonds, chopped

150 g slivered pistachios, chopped

yellow, green and pink or red food colouring

tiny bunches of green grapes, to decorate (optional)

a 700-ml loaf tin

Serves 8 or more

Cut a piece of baking parchment 2½ times the length of the loaf tin. Double it for strength, then use to line the base and sides of the tin. Leave the excess paper hanging out. This helps provide leverage when removing the loaf.

Put the shelled pistachios into a heatproof bowl and cover with boiling water. Leave for 10 minutes, then drain, pat dry and remove the skins; the nuts will be a beautiful green.

Arrange neat rows of the apricots in the bottom of the loaf tin (see opposite), reserving any left over for later. Scatter in half the blanched pistachios.

Slice off one-third of the marzipan lengthways and colour it pale yellow by kneading food colouring in. Roll it out to fit the tin, then place over the apricot layer. Scatter in the remaining blanched pistachios.

Put the sugar, zest and rosewater into an electric grinder and whizz to a deep orange paste. Scrape this into a food processor, add the pine nuts and pulse to a gritty paste. Spread this mixture over the marzipan and pistachios.

Halve the remaining marzipan. Colour one portion pale green, then knead in half the chopped pistachios. Roll out to size and place in the tin. Press down firmly.

Scissor-chop the remaining apricots and scatter these into the tin with the remaining pistachios. Push down firmly.

Colour the last piece of marzipan pale pink, then roll to size and fit in the tin. Press down firmly. Fold the overhanging paper over the top of the terrine and chill for 12 hours.

Holding the ends of the baking parchment, lift the terrine out of the tin and place on a board or plate. Peel off the parchment, then use a very sharp knife to cut 1-cm slices of the terrine. Decorate each serving with a tiny bunch of grapes, if liked. Serve with afternoon tea, or use as a dessert, maybe with pistachio ice cream or scoops of a citrus sorbet.

Note: To save time, you can buy ready-coloured marzipan from the supermarket.

To drink: Chilled or deep-frozen Muscat, the latter served as a kind of sorbet.

These crisp, wafer-like pastries dusted with icing sugar are seen in pâtisseries and bakers all over Provence. They are known by different names according to the region in which they are made – *ganses*, *bugnes*, *merveilles* – but in Provence they are affectionately known as *oreillettes* (little ears). The pastry is pulled through slits cut into it to make the shape that does indeed resemble an ear. Enjoy these carnival treats at teatime or whenever they take your fancy. My version includes cardamom seeds – not traditional, but delicious nonetheless.

crisp pastry shapes
oreillettes

375 g plain white flour

2 tablespoons caster sugar

⅛ teaspoon salt

2 large, free-range eggs, beaten

60 g butter, diced, at room temperature

60 ml dark rum

20 green cardamom pods, crushed and seeds extracted

50:50 mixture of virgin olive oil and peanut oil, for frying

sifted icing sugar, for dusting

a deep-fat fryer or a large saucepan with a frying basket

Serves 6 or 8

Put half the flour into a large bowl, add the sugar and salt, and mix together. Make a well in the centre, then add the eggs, butter, rum and cardamom seeds. Mix, using a fork, until a sticky ball of dough forms. Add half the remaining flour and mix again. Add the final amount of flour and knead until smooth. Cover the dough and chill for 20 minutes.

Put a sheet of greaseproof paper on the work surface and place one-third of the dough on it. Roll it out thinly, to no more than 3 mm thick.

To make ribbons, cut the pastry into strips measuring 4 x 12 cm. Loop into U-shapes.

To make knots, roll out another third of the dough as described in step 2 and use a serrated cutter, scissors or a knife to cut strips measuring 3 x 12 cm. Tie each one into a loose knot.

To make oreillettes, roll out the last piece of dough as described in step 2 and cut out 8 ovals or rectangles about 12 cm long and 8 cm wide. Cut two parallel slashes at the opposite ends of each shape. Pull some pastry through each slit into a curve.

Heat a 15-cm depth of the oils to 180°C (350°F) in the deep-fat fryer or saucepan. Slip 3 or 4 of the pastries into the hot oil and cook for about 1½ minutes, or until crisp and golden. Turn them over and cook for another 30–60 seconds. Drain on crumpled kitchen paper while you cook the rest.

Arrange the pastries on a serving plate and dust with sifted icing sugar. Serve warm.

To drink: Tea, coffee, hot chocolate, a tisane or a tiny eau de vie.

Vanessa et François MASTO
50 SIMIANE-LA-ROTONDE · Tel 04 . 75 95 93

Banon

Poids net
100g
FERMIER
Fromage de chèvre au lait cru

Provençal sheep's and goats' milk cheeses

Of all the pleasures of doing a daily shop in the markets of Provence (normal procedure for almost all householders), the most fun is choosing some cheese for the day's meals. From a creamy *brousse* for breakfast to some *crottins de chèvre* for lunch, or a compact *brique* or *carré* of cows' milk as a snack, the choice is fantastic. In fact, many cheeses are served as a course in themselves.

For cheese lovers who have never visited Provence, the cheese they are most likely to have heard of and tasted is *Banon*, named after the town situated near Forcalquier in the Alpes-de-Haute-Provence. A whole round, flat cheese weighs about 100 g and is enclosed in chestnut leaves tied up with raffia. It seems to embody the spirit of Provence: authentically earthy, yet elegantly fragrant, with both a slight acidity and a creamy charm. Nowadays, sadly, the name 'Banon' is used to define a style of cheese sold all over Provence and worldwide, which is often inauthentic, being neither from the actual area nor made with the proper ingredients or care. To taste the real thing, seek out a *Banon de Banon*, made in the town itself.

For a true *Banon*, the milk must come from specified goat breeds grazed freely on open, but approved, local pasture land. No silage or genetically modified cereal feed is allowed to be fed to the animals. In the traditional procedure, the milk is heated, then curdled with rennin (in the past, fig leaves or wild thistle sap would have been used). The curds and whey are collected, and both are used for cheese. *Banon* curds are turned just twice by hand, then salted. The cheese is sprinkled with pepper and savory to inhibit the growth of micro-organisms, and also to aid maturation. Most cheeses are aged for 20 days, some for much longer. Classic *Banon* is wrapped in virgin chestnut leaves that have never been trodden underfoot. They are treated with vinegar or alcohol, then wrapped around the cheese and tied with raffia from Madagascar. Finally comes the maturing, conditioning and ageing of the cheese, usually in caves or cellars that have a steady low temperature and high humidity. This careful approach is well worthwhile; longer-aged *Banons* are often pungent and runny, with a nutty-sweet and herbal flavour. *Banon* cheese now has its own AOC.

In the past, true *Banon de Banon* was made in season, using ewes' milk in season and goats' milk in late summer and autumn. Pure ewes' milk versions are rarely available these days; more often a mixture of milks is used, including cows' milk.

The main types of goat used for milk in Provence are *Saanens Blanches*, *Alpines Chamoisées* and *Communes*. The shaggy red-haired *Le Rove*, a sharp-horned breed, is also highly valued. The sheep used for milk are often Merinos and Merino cross-breeds. Some milk comes from the cattle in the Camargue, but it goes mainly into *tommes* – large, pressed, matured discs of cheese which are sometimes fashioned into *gardians*, named after the local cattlemen of the region – and the whey by-produce, *brousse*.

Left: There is a bewildering variety of Provençal cheeses in a range of shapes, sizes and textures. The most famous cheeses come from Banon in the Alpes-de-Haute-Provence region.

Some so-called *gardian* cheeses come from the Dauphiné region, but they are in fact industrial, pasteurized cows' milk cheeses, and best avoided. The same applies to any so-called *Banons* from the Dauphiné, especially those coated with cumin seeds, curry, paprika, peppercorns, rosemary, *fines herbes* or *herbes de Provence*.

Of the numerous local cheeses still flourishing in rural areas, some noteworthy ones include *chevrotine*, *Pélardon*, *brousse*, *crottins de chèvre*, *tomme de chèvre*, *tomme fraîche* and *Froumai gras*. These small or large drum-shaped cheeses are made from a mixture of cows' and ewes' milk. Pungent products made from local milks, such as *cachat* (also known as *chacheia* or *cacheille*) and the potted cheese mix called *fromage fort de Mont Ventoux*, are also famous. The latter is strong enough for maggots to thrive in it, but they are killed off when the cheese is served grilled on croûtes. Camargue cheeses include Le Camarguais, *pure brebis*, *brebis-chèvre* and *tomme de Camargue*.

Cheese of one milking may appear in many forms, including *crottins* (small round 'droppings'), *rigottes* (cylinders), *bûchettes* (logs), *chapelets* (like strings of beads), *pyramides* (flattened pyramids), *coeurs* (hearts) and *birettas* or *cardinals* (shaped like ecclesiastical hats). Some are pressed into straw-lined moulds, while others are leaf-layered in earthenware pots, or preserved in glass jars and coated with oil, ground pepper, herbs, eau de vie or liqueur (such as Frigolet), or brine. Cheeses matured for longer, such as *tommes*, are usually shaped as *briques* or *pavés* (slabs). These often have a mellower, nuttier flavour, a denser paste and a thicker, yellowish crust.

confits, boissons et frivolités
preserves, drinks and treats

black jam
confiture noir

Who could not be intrigued by the idea of jam containing aubergine? This recipe uses black fruit for its pectin, colour and scentedness, and aubergines for bulk.

400 g aubergines, trimmed and cubed
350 g black plums, stoned and cubed
300 g black seedless grapes, halved, and 300 g blueberries
150 g blackberries
600 g preserving sugar (sugar with pectin)
freshly squeezed juice of 2 lemons, plus their zest coarsely grated and blanched
200 ml dry white wine or cider
250 g walnut halves or pieces

4 x 300-g jam jars with lids, sterilized (see note below)
preserving pan or wide, heavy-based saucepan

Makes 4 x 300-g jars

Put the aubergines, fruit and sugar into the preserving pan. Add the lemon juice and wine, stir well and bring to a rolling boil. Cook, stirring often, for 10 minutes. Reduce the heat to medium and cook for 15 minutes more, stirring now and then.

After 25 minutes, stir in the walnuts and zest. Cook for 5 minutes more, stirring often. Test for readiness: a sugar thermometer should register just under 110°C (230°F), and a spoonful of jam left for 2 minutes on a cold saucer should form a skin.

Stir again. Pour into the prepared jars, let cool, then seal and label. Store in a cool, dark place and use within 6 months.

Note: To sterilize jars and lids, immerse for several minutes in boiling water, then drain and dry in a moderate oven. To sterilize muslin, immerse in boiling water, leave to drip, then allow to air-dry.

melon conserve
marmelade de melon

Cavaillon is undeniably the melon centre of Provence. Author and gastronome Alexandre Dumas once made a pact with the town elders to donate some of his books to the local library in return for some of their sweetest melons. Maybe he enjoyed melon jam like this one.

1.25 kg cantaloupe or other orange-fleshed melon
250 g preserving sugar (sugar with pectin)
freshly squeezed juice of 2 lemons (120 ml)
1 vanilla pod, split in half lengthways
1 cinnamon stick, halved
2 teaspoons eau de vie, marc or grappa

2 x 300-g jam jars with lids, sterilized (see note below)
preserving pan or wide, heavy-based saucepan

Makes 2 x 300-g jars

Quarter the melon, remove the seeds and skin, and cut the flesh into 2-cm chunks. There should be 800–850 g prepared weight. Put the melon, sugar and lemon juice into the preserving pan, stir well, then let stand for 2 hours.

Add the vanilla pod and cinnamon stick to the fruit, which by now will have become syrupy. Bring the pan to the boil and stir constantly over high a heat for 5 minutes. Reduce the heat to medium and let simmer for 15–20 minutes, stirring occasionally.

When the jam reaches nearly 110°C (230°F) on a sugar thermometer, put a tablespoonful of it on a chilled saucer; if the surface wrinkles after 5 minutes, it is ready.

Pour or ladle the hot jam into the sterilized jars. Add a teaspoonful of eau de vie to each pot. Let cool, then seal and label. Store in a cool, dark place and use within 6 months.

salt-pickled lemons
citrons confits au sel

Handsome jars of pickled lemons can often be seen in street-corner snack bars and outdoor markets throughout Provence, especially in areas that are home to North African immigrants. In fact, pickled lemons, along with harissa paste, are now popular ingredients on local menus. The salt-sharp taste is strangely appealing. Use just the skin, discarding the pith and flesh, and serve with lamb or mutton stews and tagines, fish dishes and couscous.

16 fresh, ideally unsprayed lemons, scrubbed and dried
200 g coarse sea salt or rock salt
12–16 hot, dried red chillies

a 1.4-litre glass jar with lid, sterilized (see note, page 145)
melted paraffin wax (from chemists)

Makes 1 x 675-ml jar or 2 smaller ones

Squeeze the juice from 8 of the lemons and set aside.

Make a deep criss-cross cut at the nipple end of the remaining lemons. Extend it to 3 cm from the opposite end.

Spread 6 tablespoons of the salt in the bottom of the jar. Open each lemon and stuff with 2 tablespoons of the remaining salt. Hold them closed and push into the jar with the uncut ends down. Pack the lemons tightly together, adding the chillies at intervals and sprinkling with the remaining salt.

Pour in the reserved lemon juice: it should cover the lemons completely. (If necessary, top up with cold boiled water.)

To seal the jar, melt some paraffin wax in a bowl set over boiling water, then pour a layer on top as a seal. Leave to set hard.

Fasten the lid tightly, then leave to mature in a cool, dark place for 2–3 weeks, or up to 2 months.

Note: Remove the lemons using tongs or a metal fork rather than your fingers.

anchovy paste
pissalat

Home-made jars of this strong-tasting, brownish-grey anchovy paste are still sometimes sold in the fish markets of coastal Provence. It may go by several names. *Pissalat* is what we found in Nice, while in Martigues it was called *le mélet*. It is made mainly from tiny sprats, sardines or anchovies, which are layered with sea salt, ground pepper, bay leaves and dried fennel seed heads. Covered and left in a cool place, it matures for two or three weeks, the salt helping to dissolve the bones. Once uncovered, the fish are drained, crushed and sieved. The resulting paste is a versatile condiment that can be used on hot toast, spread over the base of pizza or *pissaladière*, or used to season beef casseroles.

1 kg coarse salt
1 kg fresh small fry or anchovies, washed and drained
24 fresh bay leaves, washed, dried and lightly crushed
8 tablespoons black peppercorns, crushed
4 handfuls of dried fennel twigs and/or seed heads
4 tablespoons extra virgin olive oil

1 large glass or earthenware bowl
4 x 100-g glass jars with lids, sterilized (see note, page 145)

Makes 4 small jars

Spread a quarter of the salt in the glass bowl, then a quarter of the fish. Add 6 bay leaves, 2 tablespoons of the peppercorns and a handful of fennel. Make 3 more layers like this.

Press a heavy weight on top (wrapped in clingfilm, if metal). Cover the bowl loosely and leave for 2–3 weeks in a cool, dark place or the fridge.

Drain off and reserve any liquid. Discard the bay leaves and fennel. Put batches of the fish in a food processor and whizz to a mush. Rub through a fine, ideally nylon, sieve. Stir in the olive oil and some salty fish liquid, from earlier. Put into the sterilized jars, then seal and label. Store somewhere cool, or refrigerate.

Note: When time is tight and no pissalat is available, Patum Peperium or Gentleman's Relish may be used instead.

potted cheese paste with marc
fromage fort au marc

Maurice Duault, a long-deceased Breton friend, taught me this recipe 30 years ago. I still use it with pleasure and think of him every time. His version used Roquefort and cognac, but Provençal versions tend to be made with matured goats' cheese or sheep's milk cheese, and some *tomme* (dense alpine cow's milk cheese), grated, with butter or olive oil, seasonings, pepper or chilli flakes and some intense, dried mountain herbs. Alcohol is added to flavour and preserve it. This paste is glorious as a larder stand-by. Try it on toast, on cheese crackers as an hors d'oeuvre, on crusty baguette with lots of mesclun and tomatoes or in little pastry cases to accompany some chilled Muscat wine.

Put the 3 cheeses into a food processor and add the peppercorns. Put the butter and water in a saucepan and heat briefly over a low heat, then stir in half the eau de vie.

With the machine running, drizzle in the butter liquid and pulse to a paste. Drizzle in most of the remaining eau de vie and pulse to a slightly creamier paste. Do not overprocess.

Use a spatula to pack the paste into 1 or more of the prepared jars. Smooth the top and drizzle in the remaining eau de vie.

Cover and label the jars, then store in a larder or fridge; the paste will keep indefinitely. Remove portions with a clean spoon, then smooth the surface again.

300 g dryish, matured goats' cheese or sheep's milk cheese, grated or finely sliced

100 g Roquefort or other strong blue cheese

100 g tomme cheese, coarsely grated or sliced

1 tablespoon white peppercorns, freshly crushed or ground

50 g salted butter, cubed

4 tablespoons boiling water

4 tablespoons eau de vie de marc, branda or cognac

1 x 500-g jam jar or 4 x 125-g jars, all with lids, sterilized (see note, page 145)

Makes 1 x 500-g jar or 4 x 125-g jars

orange wine
vin d'orange

This is not a wine at all – more a decoction of citrus fruits, aromatics, wine and sugar, with the earthy boost of *alcool blanc* (white alcohol). (The better-known ratafia is a similar sort of tipple.) If making this in January, when bitter Seville oranges are available, do use them. If not, use 8 ordinary oranges, and increase the lemons to 4. Offer this as a *digestif* with coffee after a meal, or as an unusual celebratory tipple with crisp biscuits.

6 unsprayed, untreated oranges

4 unsprayed, untreated bitter oranges, such as Seville

2 unsprayed, untreated lemons

16 cloves, lightly bruised

1.5 litres alcool pour fruits 40º or other flavourless, white alcohol

4 litres dryish white or rosé wine, ideally Provençal

600 granulated white sugar

a 5-litre plastic flagon (wide-mouthed), a length of muslin, a nylon sieve, a funnel, and 7 or 8 wine bottles, all sterilized (see note, page 145)

Makes about 5–6 litres

Wash and dry the citrus fruits. Press and roll them to help release the juices. Score the skins all over, using a zester, and retain the orange zest. Quarter the fruits. Put them into the flagon with the cloves. Add 4 tablespoons of grated orange zest. Pour in half the white alcohol and 3.5 litres of the wine.

Put the remaining 500 ml wine into a saucepan with the sugar. Heat gently, stirring until completely dissolved. Cool completely over ice. Pour this syrup into the flagon. Part-seal by putting the cap or cork at an angle. Wrap clean muslin around it and secure with string.

Store in a cool, dry, dark place, and agitate the contents 3 or 4 times a day every day for a month by tilting the container.

After 30 days, strain the liquid through a muslin-lined nylon sieve. Add the remaining 750 ml white alcohol and stir. Use the funnel to transfer the liquid to the wine bottles, then seal with clean corks. Label each bottle with name and date.

The orange wine can be drunk immediately, or stored indefinitely. Once broached, store opened bottles in the fridge.

four-fruit ratafia
ratafia de quatre fruits

This delightful, ruby-red drink is best made when berry fruits are most plentiful. Since cherries are an essential component, however, their season may dictate the timing; if blackberries have not yet come into season, you could substitute loganberries or boysenberries instead. Vanilla pods and cinnamon sticks provide a fragrant boost. Use this as the basis for a kir, or mix with robust red wine.

1 kg cherries, washed and stems removed

1 kg raspberries

1 kg redcurrants or blackcurrants, washed and trimmed

1 kg blackberries, hulled

2 cinnamon sticks, lightly crushed

2 vanilla pods, slit lengthways and lightly crushed

500 g granulated white sugar

about 1 litre eau de vie, such as marc de Provence or grappa

a funnel, a 5-litre flagon (wide-mouthed), a length of muslin, a nylon sieve and a very large bottle with cork, all sterilized (see note, page 145)

Makes 2–2.5 litres

Stone half the cherries. Crush and break open some of the stones (the kernels will impart an almond flavour).

Combine all the cherries and the kernels with the raspberries, redcurrants and blackberries in a very large, non-metallic bowl. Add the cinnamon and vanilla pods. Crush everything thoroughly using a clean potato masher, wooden spoon or mallet.

Sprinkle on the sugar. Crush again and stir. Spoon the ingredients through a funnel into the prepared flagon. Part-seal by putting the cap or cork at an angle. Cover with clean muslin and secure with string. Let mature in a cool, dark, dry place for 30 days.

Strain the juices through a muslin-lined nylon sieve into a clean bowl. Measure the liquid and add the same volume of eau de vie. Pour into the large bottle, then seal with a cork. Shake gently. Store in a cool, dark place, labelled with the name and date. Drink within 1 year.

lemon verbena tea
thé de verveine

Herbalists, naturopaths, gourmands and Provençal gardeners have used the leaves of the lemon-scented verbena shrub for centuries: the aroma and taste are sharp but refreshing. Drink this infusion in the morning as a restorative after rich or spicy food the night before, or whenever you need an exhilarating lift of the spirits.

a handful of dried lemon verbena leaves or
half a handful of fresh ones, crushed
4 slices of lemon or lime
4 white sugar lumps

Serves 4

Warm a teapot. Add the leaves and top up with near-boiling water. Leave to stand for 3–5 minutes. Put a lemon slice and a sugar lump into 4 tea glasses or cups. Pour in the tea and drink hot.

Note: This tea can also be made directly in the cup. Cooled and served over ice, it makes a refreshing summer drink.

lime blossom tea
thé de tilleul

In June and July in the Drôme region you may notice people with baskets gathering the fuzzy yellow blossom from lime trees (*Tilia platyphyllos*). The tea made from it is said to promote sleep and good digestion, and to be a remedy for migraine. It also tastes delicate and delightful. Why not try it and see?

a handful of fresh lime blossoms, crushed, or half
a handful of dried lime tea
4 teaspoons wildflower honey
4 stems dried liquorice twigs (optional)

Serves 4

Put the lime blossoms in a saucepan, add 400 ml water and heat until nearly boiling. Turn off the heat and infuse for 3–4 minutes.

Put a teaspoon of honey into 4 tea glasses or cups and strain in the tea. Stir with liquorice twigs (if using) and drink hot.

pastis

With its intense yellow colour, aniseed and liquorice aromas, and sweet, spicy herbaceousness, pastis is a perfect Provençal tipple – full of sunshine, shadow and complexity. It is the drink of choice for many Provençals.

Pastis means 'mixed' or 'confused' in the Provençal dialect, and alludes to the drink's murky appearance when mixed with water. According to many Marseillais, pastis was created by a curious and inventive monk researching an elixir of life in his monastery kitchen. But folklore attributes the invention of pastis to a hermit who lived in the forest in Luberon in southern Côte du Rhône. He collected medicinal and culinary herbs, which he brewed up in a giant pot. The liquids left in the cauldron after boiling apparently had remarkable properties, providing protection from infections, as well as quenching thirst. This was put to the test when an outbreak of plague threatened the population of Luberon. The generous hermit shared his mixture with sufferers, who immediately recovered. Soon afterwards, so legend has it, he moved to Marseilles and opened a bar, which he called Au Bonhomme Passe-soif (the good-natured thirst-quencher). The last part of this name was Latinized to *passe-sitis*, and gradually evolved into the word *pastis*. This most unlikely but popular story has been handed down for generations.

A less picturesque but more feasible reason for Provence being the home of pastis is that many aromatic herbs and flowers, berries and fruits, and other curative ingredients grew wild around the villages and were thus easy to obtain. Most farmers made their own wines at this period, and distilled their own potent liqueurs. In fact, until recently the right of distillation was a family asset that could be passed from father to son. Some families still distil their own strong *pastis maison* and *branda*. Most, however, buy commercial pastis produced by the likes of Pernod Ricard, one of the biggest distilling companies in the world, or small producers, such as Henri Bardouin of Forcalquier. Pastis 51 is the leading brand, but all are made with star anise, anethol, liquorice, dill, fennel, peppercorns, cardamom, sage, nutmeg, cloves, sugar, various herbs, such as mugwort and mint, and up to 60 other possible components, as well as alcohol.

Pastis, usually a clear yellow, should be served chilled but without ice, and mixed 5 parts water to 1 part pastis. The cloudy drink that results has been nicknamed *le véritable lait de Provence* (the real milk of Provence). In a bar, Provençals ask for a *jaune* (yellow) or a *pastaga*, perhaps *flanc* (neat) or *momie* (a half measure), or a '102', which means a double Pastis 51. It is also common practice to make pastis cocktails by mixing the liqueur with local syrups and flavourings. Some recipes for these appear opposite.

pastis cocktails
coctels de pastis

Every bar in even the tiniest village in France has a rainbow array of brightly coloured, fascinatingly labelled syrups, essences, flavourings, ratafias and liqueurs. Some are alcoholic, some not. Most are sweet. The cocktails made by combining these things with pastis seem to match the many salty, earthy, aniseedy and astringent flavours of the local aperitif foods, such as capers, olives, anchovies, Aïoli (see page 15), *bacalao*, *saucissons* and artichoke hearts. Treat yourself to one of the well-known pastis cocktails below and you are instantly transported to a hot pavement under plane trees as the sun goes down – a real taste of the Mediterranean.

coctel Mauresque

2 shots pastis (Ricard, Casanis, Pernod, Berger Blanc, etc.)
2 shots orgeat or other almond syrup
ice (optional)

Serves 2

Mix together the pastis and syrup in a jug and stir well. Pour into 2 shot glasses and add ice if you wish.

coctel Perroquet

2 shots pastis
2 shots Peppermint Get (or other peppermint cordial or syrup)
ice (optional)

Serves 2

Mix together the pastis and cordial in a jug and stir well. Pour into 2 shot glasses and add ice if you wish.

the wines of Provence

When describing his beloved Provence, the painter Paul Cézanne (1839–1906) once noted that '...the sun is already warming the earth and yet the air remains sharp and dry and even tasty, like a wine. The air smells of honey, thyme, lavender, all the herbs of the nearby hills.' The Provençal landscape was evidently an inspiration to him, and so it was to the Phoenicians, who are thought to have introduced grape vines to the region in the 6th century BC. The towns of Massilia (Marseilles), Athenopolis (St Tropez), Antipolis (Antibes) and Nikaia (Nice) were the primary areas from which wine production developed.

Greeks from Phocis planted vines early in Provence, including syrah. It is believed that this great grape came from the Phocaean town of Shiraz (now in Iran), then the epicentre of wine growing in Asia Minor. The Romans, who added Provence to their empire in the 2nd century BC, continued grape cultivation there, especially at the northern end of the Rhône valley – the Côte Rôtie near Vienne, and Hermitage near Valance. In fact, both areas are still famed for the quality of their wines.

After the Romans departed, vine cultivation dwindled into obscurity. It was revived during the 9th century AD when the Church acquired large tracts of wine territory. By 1309, Clement V, the first of the Avignon popes, gave his name to a brilliant Bordeaux wine: Château Pape-Clément. The vineyards near his new summer residence, Châteauneuf-du-Pape, between Avignon and Orange, became so famous for their superb wines that some historians give this as a (tongue-in-cheek) reason why so many papal dignitaries were loath to return to Rome.

The wines of Provence have had a very chequered history: periods of glory interspersed with periods of decline. Until the 19th century, the region was second only to Bordeaux as the biggest wine-exporting centre in France. But disaster struck in the 1860s, when its vines succumbed to the deadly *Phylloxera vastatrix*, a disease carried by a tiny insect indigenous to North America. Two-thirds of French vineyards were hit, and it was feared that the industry would never recover. However, research revealed that by grafting European vines onto North American rootstocks the vine could be protected against this scourge. This gave new hope and life to the French wine industry, and helped restore the glory of Provence's vine-growing landscape.

Many vineyards were planted during World War I, and these continue to flourish. With the exception of the Côteaux des Baux around Les Baux, and the Côtes de Provence in the Var *département*, the best wines of southern Provence, in the opinion of many experts, come from along the coast.

In recent decades, increased state aid, combined with advances in technology and the help of 'flying wine-makers' from the New World, has brought new life to Provence's wine industry. The region is now best known for its rosés and affordable VDQS (Vins Délimités de Qualité Supérieure) – wines of good quality, but not as good as those denoted AOC (Appelation d'Origine Controlée). In fact, Côtes de Provence joined the rarefied club of AOC holders in 1977, and it now has seven distinct AOC regions. In addition, the quality of its *vins de table* (everyday wines) has also improved so much over recent years that many of them are becoming sought after. Their lusty charm suits much more than the local cuisine.

The reputation of Provence's wines, while founded on ancient and respected traditions, owes a huge debt to the *terroir* itself – the interaction between vine, terrain, soil and microclimate. Growers exploit this natural advantage to the maximum, producing rosé and white wines that are brilliantly fresh, dry and fruity, with an elegant suppleness and finesse, and reds that are bursting with lush floral and berry notes, or with an intense, tannic robustness.

Côtes du Rhône AOC
Some of France's best and most famous wine comes from the vineyards of the northern Rhône. The most celebrated are Côte Rôtie and Hermitage. Once past Montélimar and properly into Provence, the best wines are to be found in the villages around the Dentelles, notably Gigondas, and at Châteauneuf-du-Pape. To the west are the light, pleasant, but not remarkable wines of the Côtes du Ventoux and the Côtes du Luberon appellations.

This southern part of the extensive Rhône valley area around Orange and Avignon produces superb wines for the money. Excellent examples can be found almost anywhere in the region, from Avignon to Vienne. Most Côtes du Rhône wines are red, with the Grenache grape being most predominant, but Grenache-Shiraz-Mourvèdre blends are thriving. Côtes du Rhône white and rosé wines are especially good with the region's foods.

Côtes du Rhône-Villages designates a smaller subdivision within the Côtes du Rhône region. It has stricter criteria and produces a superior-quality Côtes du Rhône. There are 16 villages historically recognized: Gard, Chusclan, Laudun, St-Gervais, Vaucluse, Sablet, Séguret, Roaix, Valréas, Visan, Drôme, Rochegude, Rousset-les-Vignes, Vinsobres, Rasteau, which produces the favourite sweet wine within Provence, and Beaumes-de-Venise, the last being where the world's best-loved Muscat wine comes from.

Côtes de Provence AOC
This principal appellation stretches from Marseilles across central and southern Var to the Alpes-Maritimes and Côte d'Azur. From

Toulon to Fréjus, red clay soils predominate, while the northern hills and high plains are mainly chalky. The vineyards therefore grow on limestone soils around the Maures. The grapes used are Cinsault, Grenache, Mourvèdre, Syrah and Tibouren.

The annual wine output is 160 million bottles, of which an astonishing 80 per cent are rosé. Many have the aroma of pink grapefruit and red fruits. Best drunk young, these wines make perfect *apéros* (aperitifs), and are good with salads, goats' and ewes' milk cheeses, olives and anchovies.

Bandol AOC

The historic town of Bandol is on the Mediterranean coast, west of Toulon, and its vineyards stretch along the sunny southern slopes. Rocky limestone soils predominate, and the favoured grape varieties are Mourvèdre (50 per cent), Cinsault and Grenache. Some 5 million bottles are produced annually, predominantly spicy reds and crisp, full-bodied whites, but also distinctive tawny rosés.

Red Bandol, a round, balanced and full-bodied wine, is made from the Mourvèdre grape and aged in *foudres* (oak casks) for 18 months. It ages gracefully and tends to have a rich cinnamon and black-fruits aroma, excellent with red meats and game. It is one of Provence's premier reds.

Bandol rosé is aged for eight months or longer in wood, untypical for a rosé. As a result, it has an unusual orange tint.

Bellet AOC

Wines from Bellet have always had great cachet. This tiny appellation is hidden away in the hills behind Nice and only a handful of producers remains. Bellet is produced in red, white and rosé by only two vineyards, but a recent report claimed that only one was still productive.

Several grape varieties are grown here: Rolle, Chardonnay, Pignerol, Muscadet, Mayorquin and Bourboulenc for white wines; Fuella, Braquet, Cinsault and Grenache for reds and rosés. The reds, which are crisp with elegant and balanced vanilla notes, often keep well. They suit game, red meats and aged cheeses. The rosés have an aromatic and pleasant finish, good with pink meats, young cheeses and exotic dishes. The whites, often honeyed, suit shellfish and other seafood, poultry and light meat dishes.

Production is small – only 80,000 bottles – so Bellet wine is almost impossible to buy, even in and around Nice.

Coteaux d'Aix-en-Provence AOC

The Coteaux d'Aix-en-Provence received its AOC rating relatively recently, in 1985. Superior grape types plus careful handling of its vinification and ageing have led to some charming vintages. About 70 per cent of the production is rosé.

Both rosé and red wines are made from Grenache, Cinsault, Syrah, Counoise, Mourvèdre, Carignan and Cabernet Sauvignon grapes. The few white wines produced are made from the Rolle, Ugni Blanc, Clairette, Sauvignon Blanc, Bourboulenc, Grenache and Sémillon grape varieties.

Coteaux de Baux-de-Provence AOC

Situated at the base of the Alpilles, the Baux region has chalky limestone soil rich in bauxite, which imparts a distinctively austere character to the wines produced. The grape varieties used are Grenache, Cinsault, Syrah, Mourvèdre, Carignan and Cabernet Sauvignon. As an added bonus, much of the cultivation here is organic, using no artificial fertilizers or pesticides.

Red wines comprise 70 per cent of the region's output, with rosé making up the rest. Both benefit from being aged for five or six years.

Cassis AOC

Among the rocky inlets of the Mediterranean coast to the east of Marseilles sits Cassis, which has long been renowned for its white wines. These are produced from various grape varieties, including Clairette Blanc, Ugni Blanc, Marsanne, Bourboulenc, Sauvignon Blanc and Pascal Blanc. Reds and rosés are made from Grenache, Cinsault, Mourvèdre, Carignan and Barbarou grapes.

The whites, delicately nutty in flavour and the colour of tawny straw, marry well with the region's excellent seafood. The Blanc de Blancs is especially fine.

Coteaux Varois AOC

Many good vineyards can be found in the Coteaux Varois. Most wines are produced around the Var, particularly near to Brignoles. This is a very new AOC, having received its classification in 1993. Although some of the local red wines are earning plaudits, the whites and rosés are less well known outside the area.

About 70 per cent of the wines are rosé, made from Grenache, Cinsault, Syrah, Mourvèdre, Tibouren and Carignan grapes. All these varieties, apart from Tibouren, are also used to make reds. The small quantity of white wines made in this area use Clairette, Grenache, Rolle, Ugni Blanc, Sémillon and sometimes Viognier.

Camargue wines

Les Salins du Midi, traditionally a major salt producer, has diversified by planting over 1,600 hectares of vineyards along the Rhône delta coast from Sète, southwest of Montpellier, to the mouth of the Rhône. These vines produce some very pleasant, earthy *vins de table* including a number of fruity, crispy, refreshing whites and rosés which perfectly complement the salty, garlicky and sometimes hispanic flavours of the local meat, rice and seafood dishes.

websites

COOKING SCHOOLS

www.holidayonthemenu.com
*Based in La Cadier d'Azur near
Bandol and the coast, the
Hostellerie Bérard offers one-week
residential cooking classes and visits
to local suppliers. Has a one-star
Michelin restaurant.*

www.cuisineprovencale.com
*Cuisine et Tradition School of
Provençale Cuisine in Arles has
residential cooking classes and
French language immersion classes
for food lovers.*

www.cuisineinternational.com
*This website has links to two
Provençal cooking schools. One is in
the foothills of the Alps near Nyons
and the other on the Esterel coast
overlooking the Bay of Cannes. Both
have residential courses.*

**www.patriciawells.com/cooking/
provence.htm**
*For several weeks each year Patricia
Wells opens her 18th-century
Provençal home for personalized
cooking classes for a small number
of guests.*

www.theinternationalkitchen.com
*Links to Saint-Tropez chef Cyril
Breteau who offers one-day classes
for a minimum of 4 people. Also
links to many other schools.*

FOOD

www.confiserieflorian.co.uk
*Mail order and factory shops of
Florian: one of the best-known
suppliers of traditional Provençal
confectionery, crystallized fruit, fruit
jellies and jams, flower preserves,
confits etc.*

www.lefruitier.com/provence-shop
*Internet shop for the food of
Provence. Ships worldwide.
A wide selection including olives,
tapenades, aubergine caviar, dried
tomato caviar, olive oil, honey and
jams.*

www.atouchofprovence.com/
*USA-based internet supplier of
Provençal food and kitchen fabrics.
Also lists a Massachusetts-based
Provençal cooking school.*

**www.thefrenchybee.com/gourmet
-grocery-c-22.html**
*USA-based internet supplier of
Provençal goods including truffles,
olive oils, walnut and hazelnut oils,
Camargue sea salt, snails, honey,
nougats and Calissons d'Aix.*

www.alziari.com.fr
*Old-established and famous olive oil
producer with shop in Nice at 14 rue
Saint François de Paule.*

www.real-eating.co.uk
*Sells Nicolas Alziari Extra Virgin Olive
Oil and A L'Olivier Extra Virgin Olive
Oil, both from Nice in the Côte
d'Azur.*

www.theherbfarm.co.uk
*Laurel Farm Herbs (01728 668 223)
supplies a vast range of herbs to
your door from their farm in Sussex.*

www.beyond.fr/themes/truffles
*Provençal truffle markets; towns,
times, seasons plus general
information about truffles.*

www.thespiceshoponline.com
*The Spice Shop, 1 Blenheim
Crescent, London W11 2EE
Tel: 020 7221 4448
Dried herbs, spices, blends, grains,
nuts and fruits.*

www.chocmail.co.uk
*Supplier of Valrhona 'Grand Cru'
chocolates.*

**www.chocosphere.com/Html/
Products/valrhona.html**
*USA-based supplier of all Valrhona
chocolate products.*

www.mycologue.co.uk
*The internet mushroom shop. A
unique selection of products that will
delight everyone interested in
collecting, eating, cultivating or just
appreciating mushrooms. You'll also
find useful information and great
links, including mushrooming
holidays in France.*

www.fortnumandmason.com
*Fortnum & Mason, 181 Piccadilly,
London, W1A 1ER
Stocks Banon cheese and a wide
range of foodstuffs.*

USEFUL INFORMATION

www.provenceweb.fr
*Full of information on markets,
festivals, villages, hotels, restaurants
and much, much more. A must for
planning any visit to Provence.*

www.provenceguide.com
*General guide to Provence with
sections on food and wine.*

www.provencebeyond.com
*Source for travel in Provence, with
maps, travel information, hotels, and
detailed sections on villages,
gastronomy, wine, etc.*

**www.whatsonwhen.com/pages/
provence.jml**
*Dates and places of festivals,
exhibitions and food fairs throughout
Provence.*

www.villedementon.com
*Website of the town of Menton with
sections on its unique lemon festival
and the gastronomy of the area.*

Escoffier Museum of Culinary Art
*In the house where Auguste
Escoffier, France's most famous
cook, was born.*
3, Rue Auguste Escoffier
06270 Villeneuve-Loubet Village
Tel: 04.93.20.80.51
Fax: 04.93.73.93.79
www.fondation-escoffier.org

**www.coeurduvar.com/moulins/
ukdoc.htm#0**
*Lists two working olive oil mills that
can be visited, one traditional and
one modern.*

WINE AND SPIRITS

www.bbr.com
*Berry Bros & Rudd (0870 900
4300). Long-established London
wine merchant with tremendous
expertise and a large list including
such wines as Picpoul de Pinet.*

www.wine-searcher.com
*Search engine for finding suppliers
of French wines in the UK and USA.*

**www.beerliquors.com/buy/liquors/
pastis.htm**
*USA-based supplier of pastis
(Pernod, Ricard) and absinthe.*

index

acknowledgements

A fond dedication to our beloved friend, colleague and inspirer, the late
Elsa Petersen-Schepelern, whose company we sadly missed, especially during the
photography which took place all over Provence.

Special thanks to my husband, Ian Ferguson, for his thorough research, assistance
and constant support. Our Provençal forays together were always enchanting fun.

To designer Enrica Stabile, who kindly allowed us to photograph this book at her
Provençal home, Le Mas de la Rose in Le Thor, grateful thanks. La Mas de la Rose
is available to rent and details can be found on www.provenceweb.fr in the Vaucluse
section. For information on Enrica's interior decoration business, L'Utile e il
Dilettevole, see www.utile-dilettevole.it.

Thanks to Peter Cassidy for the outstanding photography and Steve Painter for his
inspired design; but even more for their convivial teamwork when we created the
images together at Le Mas de la Rose.

To assistants Marianne Lumb, Sam Kilgour, Mary Helen Trent, Debbie Dalgleish,
my thanks. Our gratitude also to Bryce and Linda Attwell, for frequent hospitality,
advice and suggestions; also to Paola Rossin, Tommi and Oli, my favourite
dégustateurs. I am thankful for Joan Minogue's kitchen; the assistance of Henry
Alexander, Judy Boulton-Lea, Alex Suter, Liz Spicer, Bernadette Lassallette and the
27th edition of *La Cuisine Provençale*, by J-B Reboul, which was so invaluable as a
tried and tested reference manual.

Thanks to Chris Losh for his interesting wine matches for my recipes.